Building faith in the
Christadelphian community.

CW00432920

TIDINGS

Volume 86, Number 10 / November, 2023

IN THIS ISSUE

Editorial—The Lord is in This Place, **Dave Jennings** 2

Life Application—Adaptation of the Ecclesia, **Trimal Accra** 8

Prayer—Abba! Father!, **Duncan Kenzie** 14

Exhortation and Consolation—He is Risen, **Russ Brierly** 19

Music and Praise—The Time of Singing has Come, **Jessica Gelineau** 26

Bible Studies — Words I Hope I Never Hear Again (3), **David Levin** 32

—Getting to Know our God and Jesus (2), **Sue and Jim Styles** . . .37

First Principles —Preaching First Principles in a Post-Christian World (2),

Richard Morgan 42

—In Whose Name?, **Melinda Flatley** 47

History—We All Love Bible Schools, **Ken Sommerville** 54

Book Review—*Christ Before Creeds*, reviewed by **Chris Sales** 61

Preaching and Teaching—A Baptism in Cuba!, **Jim Hunter** 63

—Truth Corps 2023, **Cassie Giordano** 64

—Truth Corps in Jamaica, **Dana Kohlman** 67

—How I Came to the Truth: Guatemala, **Dan Robinson** 69

THE LORD
IS IN
THIS PLACE

By Dave Jennings

DOES God ever feel distant from you? Do you find there are times when you struggle to find Him in your life? You are not alone. All of us struggle at times, deeply yearning to be closer to Him. We may struggle to take Him along with us on Monday when we return to work. Is He the Master of Sunday, or all seven days per week? In this editorial, we will suggest that evidence exists to assure our hearts that God is present, nearby, and accessible every day and in every aspect of life. Further, He understands our need for assurance and provides us with evidence of His surrounding love. He doesn't want us to seek Him in the dark.

David learned through all of his trials that wherever he found himself, God was with him. Whether hiding in a cave, running for his life, or facing the giant on the battlefield–God was his only abiding place. He writes:

He that dwelleth in the secret place of the most High shall abide under the shadow of the Almighty. I will say of the Lord, He is my refuge and my fortress: my God; in him will I trust. Surely he shall deliver thee from the snare of the fowler, and from the noisome pestilence. He shall cover thee with his feathers, and under his wings shalt thou trust: his truth shall be thy shield and buckler. (Psa 91:1-4).

This was a great lesson for David. Through all his life's intense victories and disappointments, he knew that God's presence was with him. When his great sin with Bathsheba and Uriah was exposed, David's plea was that God would *"cast me not away from thy presence."* (Psa 51:11).

Indeed, God reassured Joshua that as he succeeded Moses, *"I will be with thee: I will not fail thee, nor forsake thee."* The writer to the Hebrews picks up on this at the sunset of the Jewish age, just before the destruction of the Temple by the Romans. There would need to be a new way of thinking about the holy place and a new way to contemplate sacrifices. The Jewish world would indeed be turned upside down, but God provided great assurance to faithful believers.

Let your conversation be without covetousness; and be content with such things as ye have: for he hath said, I will never leave thee, nor forsake thee." (Heb 13:5) Or, as the Emphatic Diaglott translates part of this passage, *"No, I will not leave thee, no, no, I will not forsake thee."*

The temple that God chooses to dwell in was never intended to be a stone and wood structure but rather within the soft, malleable hearts of men and women. Paul, drawing from Leviticus 26:12-13, demonstrated to the Corinthians how God desired to dwell with believers:

For ye are the temple of the living God; as God has said, I will dwell in them, and walk in them; and I will be their God, and they shall be my people. (2 Cor 6:16).

But How?

It might serve us to review a few Scriptures that "operationalize" how this happens in our modern lives. How does God dwell with us? How might we know His presence? How can we see Him in all aspects of our lives?

Let's first admit that we have a feeble comprehension of how God works in our lives until well after events occur. We are often blind to the actions of the angels. If we knew all their countless ministrations for us, we would be greatly assured of His loving presence.

William Law (1686–1761), in *A Serious Call to a Devout and Holy Life*, wrote:

> Could you see all that which God sees, all that happy chain of causes and motives which are to move and invite you to a right course of life, you would see something to make you like that state you are in as fitter for you than any other. But as you cannot see this, so it is here that your Christian faith and trust in God is to exercise itself and render you as grateful and thankful for the happiness of your state as if you saw that everything that contributes to it with your own eyes.

As we look back on life, we see evidence of His presence. We discern how we were brought to our present circumstance, what we learned from experiences, and how our faith was tried, but increased. It is a profitable review, and it gives us a level of assurance. It is similar to Jacob declaring about Bethel, *"Surely the LORD is in this place; and I knew it not."* (Gen 28:16).

But is this what is meant by having God as our dwelling place? A dwelling place should be an active, present benefit. It is a place where one can take refuge during the storm, not only reflecting on it afterward.

This is my challenge, and I suspect many others may share this dilemma. I long to "see" God right before my eyes. Is this even possible?

The Lord Jesus spoke of how he and his Father would dwell with believers. It helps us to understand better the relationship they desire with us.

> *If a man love me, he will keep my words: and my Father will love him, and we will come unto him, and make our abode with him.* (John 14:23).

Now that's what I am looking for. Not an after-the-fact relationship, where I can see the Father and Son were once present by certain developments in my life, but one where I have confidence they are with me right now. How can I get there?

Bro. Harry Tennant wrote in *The Christadelphian Magazine* in 1969 about this concept of God being at home with us.

> God at home with us! How marvelously condescending is this picture of the work of God and His Son! If then we find this complex life of tensions and pressure a source of distress and of uncertainty, let us learn the lesson

We operate best when we are assured that our spouse or close friends love and care for us. God understands this need.

of living with God and see Him in every room of our lives, in every part of the day, through every window and door. So it was with Jesus who, having no permanent abode, no established residence, was more surely based than any man who has ever lived, and dwelt always with God, and God with him.

That's what I long for.

In human relationships, we long for affection, love, and acceptance expressions. We operate best when we are assured that our spouse or close friends love and care for us. God understands this need. To confirm to us, He provides evidence of how the Father and Son dwell with us.

And he that keepeth his commandments dwelleth in him, *and he in him. And hereby we know that he abideth in us, by the Spirit which he hath given us.* (1 John 3:24).

Hereby know we that we dwell in him, and he in us, because he hath given us of his Spirit. (1 John 4:13).

Jesus is not waiting at a distance for the Judgment, keeping a record of our good and evil deeds. Instead, he is right in the house! Any chastening needed he provides today to help conform us to his image now. If we keep the commandments, if we love Jesus, and if we love our brother, Jesus will progressively manifest himself to us. If we want to know whether we are dwelling with God, we need to assess how committed we are to these behaviors today.

The Apostle John seems focused on this concept of God dwelling with us through the Son.

If we love, the Father and Son will make their abode. (John 14:23).

If we abide in Jesus, the vine, we can produce fruit. (John 15:4-5).

If we confess Jesus, by love, by the Spirit, he dwells in us. (1 John 4:12-18).

The truth's sake, which dwelleth in us, shall be with us forever. (2 John 1:2).

In many of his writings, Paul also wrote about the dwelling of Jesus in the lives of believers. To the Romans, Paul said:

But ye are not in the flesh, but in the Spirit, if so be that the Spirit of God dwell in you. Now if any man have not the Spirit of Christ, he is none of his. And if Christ be in you, the body is dead because of sin; but the Spirit is life because of righteousness. But if the Spirit of him that raised up Jesus from the dead dwell in you, he that raised up Christ from the dead shall also quicken your mortal bodies by his Spirit that dwelleth in you. (Rom 8:9-11).

This passage is critical to understanding how God dwells with us. The evidence we are looking for is the quickening by the Spirit—the witness of the activity of the power of God in our lives. It represents a transforming mind that eschews unrighteous works and clings to the righteousness of God. That state of mind is not just because we willed it or had some unique spiritual strength. It is because the all-powerful and living God is fully active in us.

Any transformation of our thinking and discernment is due to the Father's power in our lives.

Paul used a financial phrase to describe the assurance that our spiritual relationship provides us.

For we that are in this tabernacle do groan, being burdened: not for that we would be unclothed, but clothed upon, that mortality might be swallowed up of life. Now he that hath wrought us for the selfsame thing is God, who also hath given unto us the earnest of the Spirit. (2 Cor 5:4-5).

The financial phrase is the word *"earnest."* Earnest money is a deposit a purchaser makes to hold the possession until it is fully claimed. We might think of it today as a promissory note. This deposit is lost in many places if the possession is not paid for in full. The Greek word for *"earnest"* is *arrabon*, which is of Phoenician origin. It is used in literature for an engagement ring. This carries the edifying picture of a bride gazing at an engagement ring on her finger, being assured her groom has promised to be one with her. This image is a marvelous way for us to think about the promise of the Spirit. Paul calls it the *"earnest expectation"* we have as we wait for the manifestation of being sons of God. (Rom 8:19). In Ephesians, he calls it the *"earnest of our inheritance until the redemption of the purchased possession."* (Eph 1:14). While we are waiting for the redemption of our body, we have a guarantee, a promissory note that we can examine. As we see the Spirit working in our lives today, it is as if we are looking at an engagement ring on our finger, reminding us of the surety that we will be redeemed.

So, how can we see our God and the Lord Jesus, as Bro. Tennant suggested, "through every window and door?" Here are a few tangible signs that God is working in our lives. Each sends you a clear message that you are being redeemed.

- You have a determination to change for the better. It is your commitment to leave ungodly behaviors behind and to pursue God's righteousness. This attitude doesn't mean you won't fail, but it means you are in a committed relationship.

- The Lord is bringing people into your life to help you improve. This insertion might include those who are there to reinforce your positive behaviors, as well as those who chasten you to change behaviors.

- People can see you are changing. We tend to be poor judges of our own behaviors and motives. When others see transformation in our lives, it indicates the Lord's hand is operating. We no longer burst out in anger. We show love and compassion to people with very different perspectives.

- You have joy in your walk with God. You are not operating out of compulsion or a sense of obligation but because serving God and our Lord Jesus Christ and serving our fellow man brings you boundless joy. See Bro. Russ Patterson's exhortation *"The Joy of Living in Christ"* in the September 2023 edition of the *Tidings*.

- Despite the barrage of challenges you face, your vision of the Kingdom and personal purpose and direction are clear. Difficult individual choices may challenge you, but the governing fundamentals for those decisions have no ambiguity.

- You have a humble, teachable, and soft heart. Our Lord can shape you and refine your thinking. You are open to loving rebukes and constructive comments from loving brothers and sisters, recognizing that you need their help.

- You can discern opportunities to serve that open in front of you– whether planned or unplanned. We are responsive to those cues because, in prayer, we have been asking for our Lord to make our way plain and use us in his service.

Our God wants us to know that He is present. We are told to draw near. (Heb 10:22). We must never consider our God inaccessible, removed, or uninterested. For through His Son, He offers to make His home with us. Why should we ever be afraid when we have the Father and Son in our home?

And Moses verily was faithful in all his house, as a servant, for a testimony of those things which were to be spoken after; But Christ as a son over his own house; whose house are we, if we hold fast the confidence and the rejoicing of the hope firm unto the end. (Heb 3:5-6).

Dave Jennings

ADAPTATION
OF THE
ECCLESIA
IN A
GROWING
WORLD

By Trimal Accra

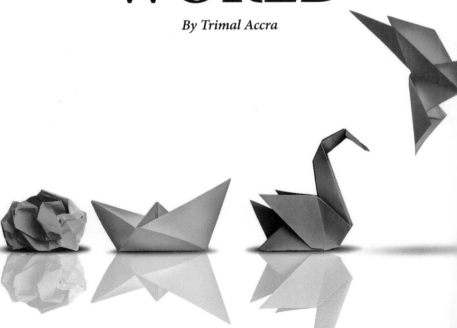

PHONES are a norm today, with almost every human owning one, whether in the form of a landline or mobile phone. However, the first phone invented was less well-liked than its modern successors. When Alexander Graham Bell invented the first telephone in 1876, it was not accepted because the telegraph had already been invented. Both devices were created to make communication as easy as possible. But because the telegraph was invented before the telephone, it was already the accepted means of communication. People were already accustomed to it.

You see, the electric telegraph had become part of the lives of many, and thus, they were not willing to accept this new technological device that Bell had invented. Even though the telegraph was impractical because it could not transmit many non-English texts and required a third party to transmit messages, people still held on to it. The major telegraph company, Western Union, rejected the new technology and even fought Bell to have his patent removed.[1]

Fast forward to 2023, and there are approximately 6.84 billion mobile phones. To put that into perspective, that number represents almost 85% of the world's 8 billion inhabitants.[2] Can you imagine a world without cell phones now? Before the telephone was created, you either had to wait for someone to inform you about something that happened or find out on your own. People were helpless in emergencies. Everything began to change when the phone network was introduced.

Today, if you miss your friends, just take a second to send them a text! Do you need an update on world news? Scroll into the BBC app. Mobile phones have made our lives so easy that without their presence today, the world would be thrown into utter chaos.

Adaptation in Nature

Before we dig into the adaptation of the ecclesia, we must first understand the concept of adaptation, and what is the best way to understand this concept than by looking at God's magnificent creation?

Adaptation is the biological mechanism by which organisms adjust to new environments or changes in their current environment. Organisms can use various strategies to adapt to their surroundings. They are capable of biological adaptation, which entails changing how the body works.

The physical characteristics of people who live in high-altitude regions like Tibet are examples of biological adaptation. The people living on the Tibetan Plateau flourish at elevations where oxygen concentrations are up to 40% lower than at sea level. Most people would become sick from breathing air that thin, but Tibetans' bodies have undergone alterations in their biological chemistry. Because their bodies produce more hemoglobin, a protein that transports oxygen in the blood, most individuals can survive at high altitudes for a brief period. Increased hemoglobin levels are not a long-term answer to high-altitude survival because they can be hazardous when present continually. Due to genetic changes, the ability to utilize oxygen much more effectively without the need for additional hemoglobin appears to exist in Tibetans.

Adapting Does Not Mean Betraying Doctrine

Now that we've had a crash course on adaptation, let us jump into the meat of our discussion. I think the greatest misconception or fear of adapting in the ecclesia is the concern that adjusting will change doctrines. It is a fair reservation to have, but it is not necessarily true.

Doctrines make us who we are, and without them, we are nothing, so they aren't something we can change. However, the ways we pray, sing, exhort, dress, and the time we start the memorial service are not resolute and thus are subject to change, causing the ecclesia to function better.

The entire premise of Christianity is based on change. God was ushering in the New Covenant; thus, the old ways of doing things were about to end. The Messiah was present in flesh and blood. The Pharisees had distorted the law so badly that they kept their own made-up laws rather than God's. Look how Jesus challenges them on this very point.

The Pharisees and some of the scribes gathered to Him after they came from Jerusalem and saw that some of His disciples were eating their bread with unholy hands, that is, unwashed. (For the Pharisees and all the other Jews do not eat unless they carefully wash their hands, thereby holding firmly to the tradition of the elders; and when they come from the marketplace, they do not eat unless they completely cleanse themselves; and there are many other things which they have received as traditions to firmly hold, such as the washing of cups, pitchers, and copper pots.) And the Pharisees and the scribes asked Him, "Why do Your disciples not walk in accordance with the tradition of the elders but eat their bread with unholy hands?" But He said to them, "Rightly did Isaiah prophesy about you hypocrites, as it is written: 'This people honor Me with their lips, but their heart is far away from Me. And in vain do they worship Me, teaching as doctrines the commandments of men. "Neglecting the commandment of God, you hold to the tradition of men." He was also saying to them, "You are experts at setting aside the commandments of God in order to keep your tradition." (Mark 7:1-9 NASB).

At first glance, we might think Jesus was allowing his disciples to break God's commandments. But quite quickly, we see that was not the case. You see, the Pharisees had many traditions and observances that, over the years, they made up and had nothing to do with God's commandments. They were not necessarily bad. In fact, washing one's hands before eating is acceptable today.

So, if this tradition was so beneficial, what exactly is the issue here? The problem was their inability to differentiate God's law from their own tradition. God's law had to be always obeyed, but their traditions did not hold much weight, and Jesus challenged them on this. They were so used to their rules that they equated them to God's laws.

It can be hard to accept new things, especially when we are so used to doing things a certain way for many years. However, we must not mistake our traditions and preferences for how something is done as God's law. So, with time, adaptations or changes may occur in non-doctrinal matters. We can sing different praise songs, we can play new instruments, we can dress differently, and we can introduce new methods and styles to our services because the end goal is to serve God at our best capacity, and that may mean making amendments because many times the old way of doing things just isn't cutting it anymore.

Two Necessary Viewpoints About Change

In everything in life, a balance must be found. Some are resistant to change, and others widely embrace it. Both kinds of people play a crucial role in maintaining the ecclesia.

Some are averse to change and see the way they did things 100 years ago as still the "best" way, often because that is what they are used to. These environments can cause those with new ideas to be stifled and afraid to speak up. In some extreme cases, they can drive a severe wedge in their relationship with God, creating resentment not only for some brothers and sisters, the ecclesia itself, and possibly even for God. This development can cause some to fall away from the faith.

In everything in life, a balance must be found.

Some are resistant to change, and others widely embrace it. Both kinds of people play a crucial role in maintaining the ecclesia.

It is time we look beyond "what we like and know" and see what works best, what is more likely to attract those outside, and what will keep our young people. If that means bringing in new methods we dislike, we must remove our biases and let the LORD's work be done.

Some are much more accepting of change, which is good if monitored closely. Trending in today's media is the movement that stemmed around gender equality and LGBTQIA2S+, where persons from these movements are calling for more acceptance. Now, while that sounds good, we know God's commands on the matter. Some can quickly turn from trying to make the ecclesia better to accepting behaviors and lifestyles that are totally against the laws of God—all under the guise of openness to change! We already see it at the community's doorsteps, and must be assessed closely.

The question now is, How do we find the balance? The answer lies in Paul's letter to the Corinthians: *"Therefore, if food causes my brother to sin, I will never eat meat again, so that I will not cause my brother to sin."* (1 Cor 8:13 NASB).

Now, what does food have to do with drawing the line? Well, everything. Paul identifies a principle that goes beyond food and shows that we should compromise for our brothers and sisters. But this still poses an issue because one group will argue that the compromise should favor their viewpoint. The two groups need to find a common ground of compromise where they learn to coexist in a Christ-like manner.

Adaptation Should Not Water Down the Truth, But Enhance It

Our motives behind wanting change are significant and must be weighed. The goal of adapting is not to look like other churches or make the ecclesia "more fun." Its main goal is simply better to facilitate service to our God and our Lord.

Adaptation can also be an effective tool in ministering the gospel to others. We can create new platforms to advertise the Truth without compromising the integrity of the Truth. So, it is not always wrong to adopt some techniques from other churches, especially when they are working, and can be adapted and modified to reach others. So, "trying an idea I heard about from my friend's church" is not necessarily bad. All that is needed is the modification to fit our doctrines. If a new method adapted from another is working and we are against it simply because it is from another denomination, we have a lot of self-assessment to do.

In the End, Change is Inevitable

When it is all said and done, change is a necessary requirement for growth, and simply put, without change, the truth may never grow.

We are responsible for seeing how we can foster healthy change for the ecclesia. We have to create platforms to discuss necessary adaptation techniques for the ecclesia. We can no longer allow ourselves to be agitated by persons bringing new instruments, creating more youth-friendly platforms, not using ties and jackets, or singing in a specific way. It is time we look beyond "what we like and know" and see what works best, what is more likely to attract those outside, and what will keep our young people.

If that means bringing in new methods we dislike, we must remove our biases and let the LORD's work be done. This compromise can only be accomplished when we sit down and put our ideas together in a loving manner that is right and fitting for brothers and sisters.

Finally, how can we foster effective and healthy ecclesial adaptation? Here are a few ideas:

1. We must recognize and eradicate our biases and traditions that hamper the ecclesia more than help it grow.

2. We must create platforms outside Bible classes or Memorial Services where both the young and old can meet and discuss matters about the growth and health of the ecclesia.

3. We must keep an open mind to new ideas, even though they may not be traditional to our ecclesia.

4. We must remember the end goal is to spread the good news to others. Sometimes, we may need to adapt our methods to teach and connect with them.

5. We must remember there is no one style of worship, no one style of prayer, no one style of dressing, and no right or wrong musical instruments–they must all be used for the glory of God.

6. And above all, we must remember always to do what's best—not for ourselves but for the ecclesia.

Trimal Accra,
Georgetown Ecclesia, Guyana

1 History.com. *"Alexander Graham Bell: Telephone & Inventions–History."* Accessed April 14, 2023 https://www.history.com/topics/inventions/alexander-graham-bell.
2 Howarth, Josh. *"How many people own smartphones (2023-2028)."* Exploding Topics. January 26, 2023. https://explodingtopics.com/blog/smartphone-stats.

ABBA! FATHER!

By Duncan Kenzie

THE The phrase *"Abba, Father"* is unique and familiar to us. But what does it mean? And how is it used in Scripture? And how can our understanding of the phrase enrich our prayer life?

It occurs only three times in Scripture, once by Jesus (Mark 14:36) in the Garden of Gethsemane, and twice by Paul (Rom 8:15, Gal 4:6). It's a strange expression because it is a combination of two languages—Aramaic (*Abba*) and Greek (Father = *o pater*). Moreover, it's a pleonasm—a phrase with built-in redundancy (the opposite of an oxymoron). This circumstance occurs because the word *"Abba"* itself means Father. So it sounds like Jesus is saying, "Father, Father." (Pleonasms are rife in the Psalms. See Psalm 18:20-24 for example. Repetition is a rhetorical device used to reinforce a message. We often hear repetition in music and poetry. So it's not surprising we find it in the Psalms, many of which we know were sung, and all of which are poetic).

Let's look at how Scripture uses the expression *"Abba, Father."* All three passages have some common elements:

1. They reference personal prayer.
2. They involve the Spirit of God.
3. They contrast freedom from sin to slavery to sin.
4. The concept of being God's Son, or sons and daughters, is integral to the context.

Galatians 4:3-7 reads,

In the same way we also, when we were children, were enslaved to the elementary principles of the world. But when the fullness of time had come, God sent forth his Son, born of woman, born under the law, to redeem those who were under the law, so that we might receive adoption as sons. And because you are sons, God has sent the Spirit of his Son into our hearts, crying, "Abba! Father!" So you are no longer a slave, but a son, and if a son, then an heir through God. (Gal 4:3-7).[1]

Like much of Galatians, this section contrasts being a slave to the law with freedom in Christ. Paul writes that God *"sent forth"* his Son to redeem those under the law. Redemption involves setting someone free and, in this case, being adopted by God as his sons and daughters (restoring to one's original family). See also Ephesians 1:3-6.

The reference to personal prayer is more oblique in Galatians 4 than in Romans 8 and Mark 14, but I think it is implicitly in the phrase, *"God has sent the spirit of his Son into our hearts, crying, 'Abba! Father!'"* The spirit of His Son is equivalent to the phrase *"the spirit of Christ"* in Romans 8:9 and 1 Peter 1:11 and to *"Christ in you"* (Col 1:27, Rom 8:10). It is the spirit of obedience to God's will that sets us free from a life enslaved to sin. When we pray earnestly and sincerely for God to work for his good pleasure with us, our hearts are crying out. It's not a ritual, rote prayer, but one that may spring from a deep struggle with our weaknesses to ask God to help us rise above them and follow our Master.

Romans 8 elaborates on these themes:

> *For if you live according to the flesh you will die, but if by the Spirit you put to death the deeds of the body, you will live. For all who are led by the Spirit of God are sons of God. For you did not receive the spirit of slavery to fall back into fear, but you have received the Spirit of adoption as sons, by whom we cry, "Abba! Father!" The Spirit himself bears witness with our spirit that we are children of God, and if children, then heirs--heirs of God and fellow heirs with Christ, provided we suffer with him in order that we may also be glorified with him. (Rom 8:13-17).*

Again, we find the same four elements in this passage that we found in Galatians 4: prayer, the Spirit of God, contrast to slavery, and becoming children of God by adoption. In this passage, Paul also compares the *"spirit of slavery"* with the *"spirit of adoption,"* demonstrating that the use of the word *"spirit"* here is primarily analogous with what we might call "mindset."

Note Paul writes that a *"spirit of slavery"* leads to fear. If we regard our relation to God as being a slave compared to a child of God, then we may tend to regard God with fear. Respect and reverence (as one would hopefully have for a worthy human father) are distinct from anxiety and are entirely appropriate for us to express to our heavenly Father. But a child who fears his father cannot truly trust him and cannot be truly honest with him. A child of God who has some understanding of God's perfect love for them will recognize that *"perfect love casts out fear"* (1 John 4:18) and will be able to express their innermost thoughts to God, drawing near to the throne of grace with reverent confidence, to receive mercy and find grace to help in time of need (Heb 10:16,19-22).

Furthermore, Paul wrote to Timothy, *"God gave us a spirit not of fear but of power and love and self-control."* (2 Tim 1:7). Thayer's Greek lexicon translates the word for *"fear"* here as timidity, fearfulness, and cowardice. God expects us to *"fear not, be of good courage"* in our struggle against sin. Anything else is cowardice.

In contrast, by the spirit of adoption, we cry, *"Abba! Father!"* In other words, because of our relationship with God, we can approach God in prayer and use this title following Jesus' instructions on how to pray: *"Our Father."* Prayer to God, like our relationship with him, is not transactional. It is not "Please God, answer my prayers, and I will do this for you." (See Exodus 24:3 for this kind of thinking). It is more "I thank you, God, for being my Father. And as such, I place my complete trust in Your care. I offer up my love, concerns, desires, and hopes, knowing that you, in your wisdom and love, will answer me according to my needs."

> *Likewise the Spirit helps us in our weakness. For we do not know what to pray for as we ought, with groanings too deep for words. And he who searches hearts knows what is the mind of the Spirit, because the Spirit intercedes for the saints according to the will of God. (Rom 8:26-27).*

There's a lot to unpack in this passage, but I think the essence is that there is a special intimacy with God when we pray with completely unfettered, open hearts and minds. From my own experience, it takes serious discipline and focus to pray with clear intention and without becoming distracted. I'm guessing that for most of us, there are often moments when we cannot find the words we want, or we have an inner conflict regarding the purpose of our prayer. We then find ourselves surrendering to God's care and presence, trusting He knows our needs even before we ask and that if we ask in inadequate ways, His grace is sufficient to compensate for our deficiencies.

This thought brings us to Mark 14:36. *"Abba, Father, all things are possible for you. Remove this cup from me. Yet not what I will, but what you will."* The context is Jesus' struggle with his human nature in the garden of Gethsemane. Again, the four common elements are present: Jesus is the Son of God, and his redemption is tied to his trusting obedience to his Father. He is engaged in earnest prayer, so serious that Luke wrote, *"And being in agony he prayed more earnestly; and his sweat became like great drops of blood falling down to the ground."* (Luke 22:44). And, further in Mark 14, we see a reference to the spirit, or mindset, of Christ: *"Watch and pray that you may not enter into temptation. The spirit indeed is willing, but the flesh is weak."* (Mark 14:38).

Jesus is the great example of how to pray with deep reverence, trust, focus, and intention. He is also a great example of how prayer can be challenging when we struggle to reconcile our desires with God's desires. The very fact Jesus said, *"Nevertheless not my will, but thine, be done"* (Luke 22:42 KJV) is a powerful witness to the plight of the human condition: we struggle to conform to God's way.

But why did Jesus use the phrase "*Abba, Father*"? You will likely have heard that "*Abba*" means "Daddy." With this translation, Jesus says, "Daddy, Father." The usual exposition is that Jesus was praying to God like a little child. This idea is charming with pleasant connotations for all of us. Perhaps we, too, can approach God our Father in prayer like a little child. But is it accurate? Several scholars propose alternative understandings. Murray Harris (1939-), a New Testament scholar who studied under F. F. Bruce, wrote this:

> It is true that in the Jewish Talmud and other Jewish documents, we find statements such as "When a child experiences the taste of wheat (i.e., when it is weaned), it learns to say 'abbā and 'immā" (Berakot 40a in the Babylonian Talmud) (= our "dada" and "mama").

> However, even if the term abba began as a childish babbling sound (and this is far from clear), at the time of Jesus, it was a regular adult word meaning "Father" or "my Father" (as terms of address) or "the Father" or "my Father" (as terms of reference).

That is, abba was not a childish term of the nursery comparable to "Daddy." It was a polite and serious term, yet also colloquial and familiar, regularly used by adult sons and daughters when addressing their father. Ideas of simplicity, intimacy, security and affection attach to this household word of childlike trust and obedience. So to bring out the sense of warm and trusting intimacy that belongs to the word, we could appropriately paraphrase it as "dear father."

If Paul had wanted to convey the sense of "Daddy," he could have used a Greek word he undoubtedly would have known–papas or pappas which means "papa" or "daddy," a child's word for "father." [2]

The key part here is that "Abba was a polite and serious term, regularly used by adult sons and daughters when addressing their fathers." The term may be "childlike," but not "childish."

And consider this excerpt from a blog post by Chad Harrington:

Washing my hands in [a restroom in Tel Aviv airport], I overheard an exchange between a Jewish father and his son.... they both knew English and Hebrew. The father said to his son (in English), "When I ask you to do something, I want you to call me Abba."

Hearing this, I was surprised by three things:

1. He was speaking in English and Hebrew in the same breath.

2. That he was using an everyday experience for child training (Good for him!).

3. The real meaning of Abba is not what I had been taught.

Most people think Abba means "Daddy," but that's not quite right. "Daddy" doesn't have the impact of Abba. It's personal, which is part of the meaning, but that's not the whole story. Abba doesn't mean "Daddy." Abba doesn't mean "Dad." Abba means "Father, I will obey you." [3]

This understanding provides a beautiful texture to the story of the Garden of Gethsemane. Jesus wasn't just addressing God affectionately. He was using a term that, despite the intense personal spiritual struggle he was experiencing, reminded him of his complete, trusting, and courageous commitment to his Father: *"Abba, Father,"* or "Father, I will obey you."

Can we find that same courage, trust, and commitment to say *"Abba, Father"* in our prayer life, with a sincere desire to obey him?

Duncan Kenzie,
Saanich Ecclesia, BC

---

1 All Scriptural citations are taken from the English Standard Version unless specifically noted.
2 Excerpt from thegospelcoalition.org/blogs/justin-taylor/why-abba-does-not-mean-daddy/.
3 Excerpt from himpublications.com/blog/meaning-abba/.

HE IS RISEN

By Russ Brierly

CONSIDER these words of Peter on the Day of Pentecost:

Men of Israel, listen to this: Jesus of Nazareth was a man accredited by God to you by miracles, wonders and signs, which God did among you through him, as you yourselves know. This man was handed over to you by God's set purpose and foreknowledge; and you, with the help of wicked men, put him to death by nailing him to the cross. But God raised him from the dead, freeing him from the agony of death, because it was impossible for death to keep its hold on him. (Acts 2:22-24 NIV).

God has raised this Jesus to life, and we are all witnesses of the fact. Exalted to the right hand of God, he has received from the Father the promised Holy Spirit and has poured out what you now see and hear. (Acts 2:32-33 NIV).

Therefore let all Israel be assured of this: God has made this Jesus, whom you crucified, both Lord and Christ. (Acts 2:36 NIV).

Peter states that Jesus of Nazareth was approved or accredited by God and that the miracles, wonders, and signs done by him were from God and performed among them **through** our Lord Jesus. He also tells us that God raised him to life again after his cruel and horrible death because the grave could not hold him. Jesus was raised to a new life that was now a spirit power, unlimited in space and time. Yet Hebrews 13:8 tells us that *"Jesus Christ is the same yesterday, today, and forever."*

If he is now unlimited in space and time, our Lord Jesus can be with each of us today. The empty tomb tells us that *"He is risen."* And if he is a risen Lord, he can be to us a saving Lord Jesus, a living Lord Jesus, and an indwelling Lord Jesus.

A Risen Lord Jesus is a Saving Lord Jesus

A risen Lord Jesus implies that he once lived, was dead, placed in a tomb, and after three days was raised to life again. Our salvation would not be possible if he had not been raised to life. Nothing that is an integral part of our being saved would be available to us today. There would be no forgiveness of sins, no justification or possibility of being made right with God, and no reconciliation or means of finding peace with God. There would be no redemption from the bondage of sin all mankind is subject to and no adoption of each of us as sons and daughters of our Father in heaven. Jesus would not be "our Lord and Savior" but one more failed Messiah.

But God's love for His only begotten Son and His love for the people He created left no room for a failed Messiah. God expresses His overwhelming love for us in John 3:16 (KJV):

> *For God so loved the world, that he gave his only begotten Son, that whosoever believeth in him should not perish, but have everlasting life.*

In John, we are told the love he had for His Father motivated Jesus to live a sinless life and then die a cruel, horrible death at the hands of murderous Roman soldiers inspired by scheming Jewish religious leaders. It was that love that kept him doing what His Father commanded. Jesus said, *"I do as the Father has commanded me, so that the world may know that I love the Father."* (John 14:31 ESV).

His sacrifice and the empty tomb, which proclaims, *"He is risen,"* set forth the reality that we can, with our repentance and belief, change our relationship with God, and by signifying our death to sin through baptism, we can begin life anew with our Lord Jesus as healer and restorer. With joy, we can know that our sins are forgiven and confidently accept that we have been justified or made right with the Father. Our Lord's sacrifice has brought about a reconciliation and helped us find peace with God. Listen to what Paul says of the freedom from sin that Christ brings.

> *But now that you have been set free from sin and have become slaves of God, the fruit you get leads to sanctification and its end, eternal life.* (Rom 6:22 ESV).

It is John who speaks to us of the wonderful experience of becoming part of the family, an experience often celebrated at a baptism with the singing of the song "Welcome to the Family." John writes of that occasion, *"But to all who did receive him, who believed in his name, he gave the right to become children of God, who were born, not of blood nor of the will of the flesh nor of the will of man, but of God."* (John 1: 12-13 ESV).

Our Lord Jesus is truly and wonderfully a saving Lord Jesus.

A Risen Lord Jesus is a Living Lord Jesus

A risen Lord Jesus is playing an active role in our lives. In Romans 5:10 we read the following words, *"We were reconciled to God by the death of his Son, much more, now that we are reconciled, shall his life save us."* (ESV) We have discussed the role that the death of his Son played in our salvation. Now we want to look at what it means to be "saved by his life," and our Lord Jesus's role in strengthening and encouraging us.

Jesus' sacrifice and the empty tomb, which proclaims, "He is risen," set forth the reality that we can, with our repentance and belief, change our relationship with God...

Consider these words from the first epistle of John: *"And this is the testimony: that God has given us eternal life, and this life is in His Son."* (1 John 5:11 NKJV). The Greek word translated as life in both instances in this passage is the same, *zoe*, and it can apply to both our lives now and in the future. Bible dictionaries convey the thoughts of a "life real and genuine, a life active and vigorous, devoted to God" and "of the absolute fulness of life, both essential and ethical." John is encouraging us to *"continue to love one another."* He goes on to state that *"love comes from God,"* and *"God has sent His only begotten Son into the world, that we might live (zoe) through Him."* (1 John 4:9 NKJV).

To grasp this concept, we must see a living, active, and loving Lord Jesus Christ, a Lord Jesus so close to us daily that we can walk beside him, accepting his yoke and letting him help carry our burdens. The Lord Jesus promised those few disciples who gathered around him that he would come to them in a different form and assured them of his presence with the words, *"Lo, I am with you always, even to the end of the age."* (Matt 28:20 NKJV).

Think for a moment about the role of the High Priest that Jesus plays now.

> *Consequently, he is able to save to the uttermost those who draw near to God through him, since he always lives to make intercession for them.* (Heb 7:25 ESV).

Also, Hebrews 2:18 assures us that he is very much a living Lord Jesus, who knows us and can help us, *"because he himself has suffered when tempted, he is able to help those who are being tempted."* (ESV). Jesus is just as desirous to intercede in our lives and help us when we are tempted as he helped Peter overcome his guilt and go on to accomplish great things to God's glory.

Paul, in a number of places, talks about the Lord Jesus giving him strength: *"I can do all things through him who strengthens me."* (Phil 4:13 ESV). Also, to Timothy, *"I thank him who has given me strength, Christ Jesus our Lord."* (1 Tim 1:12 ESV). In Ephesians, he writes about the,

> *Immeasurable greatness of* [God's] *power toward us who believe, according to the working of his great might that he worked in Christ when he raised him from the dead and seated him at his right hand in the heavenly places, far above all rule and authority and power and dominion, and above every name that is named, not only in this age but also in the one to come. And he put all things under his feet and gave him as head over all things to the church, which is his body, the fullness of him who fills all in all."* (Eph 1:19-23 ESV).

We must see a living, active, and loving Lord Jesus Christ, a Lord Jesus so close to us daily that we can walk beside him, accepting his yoke and letting him help carry our burdens

The Father has put us in the loving arms of his beloved Son, who loves and knows us. Our God is working through Jesus to encourage and strengthen...

Yahweh has elevated His Son to a high and exalted position at His right hand and placed him as head over all things. Jesus Christ is our head. The Father has put us in the loving arms of his beloved Son, who loves and knows us. Our God is working through Jesus to encourage and strengthen, to help us breathe in that zoe life that helps us see and feel his own zoe life, and through this closeness, this relationship, we can become *"saved by his life."*

The benediction to the Book of Hebrews may help sum up these thoughts and help us realize that a risen Lord Jesus is a living, active, and dynamic Lord Jesus who can be as alive to us as we allow him.

Now may the God of peace who brought again from the dead our Lord Jesus, the great shepherd of the sheep, by the blood of the eternal covenant, equip you with everything good that you may do his will, working in us that which is pleasing in his sight, through Jesus Christ, to whom be glory forever and ever. Amen. (Heb 13:20-21 ESV).

A Risen Lord Jesus is an Indwelling Lord Jesus

How would we define the word indwelling, especially when it's not directly used in Scripture? Perhaps the best way to grasp the meaning of the words is to look at a few scriptures that use the words.

When I think of all this, I fall to my knees and pray to the Father, the Creator of everything in heaven and on earth. I pray that from his glorious, unlimited resources he will empower you with inner strength through his Spirit. *Then Christ will **make his home in your hearts** as you trust in him.*" (Eph 3:14-17 NLT).

This is the power of the Father that Paul sees as empowering the believers by giving them the inner strength to grow and endure. Having been given that inner strength, Paul says, *"Then Christ will make his home in your hearts as you trust in him."* The King James Version says, *"dwell in your hearts by faith,"* but the NLT translates the Greek word pistis as *"as you trust in him,"* indicating that it's your faith or your belief in the Lord Jesus that determines whether he dwells in your heart or not.

Let's now examine the words of Jesus himself. In John 15, he speaks of the true vine and begins this section with the words, *"I am the true vine, and my Father is the vinedresser."* A branch of a vine cannot bear fruit by itself. It needs to remain connected to the vine to bear fruit. Jesus applies this agricultural principle to one's spiritual growth and sets forth the importance of the relationship if we hope to bear

fruit to the glory of the Father.

*Abide in me, and I in you. As the branch cannot bear fruit by itself, unless it abides in the vine, neither can you, unless you abide in me. I am the vine; you are the branches. Whoever **abides in me and I in him**, he it is that bears much fruit, for apart from me you can do nothing.*" (John 15:4-5 ESV).

By the way, this is a two-way relationship, as is clearly stated in the passage, *"Whoever **abides in me and I in him**, he it is that bears much fruit."* (John 15:5). Note also that Jesus states that without him **we can do nothing**. This verse serves as a reality check on what we can accomplish without our living Lord Jesus.

Consider the passages that use the words *"Christ in you."* Paul wrote, *"But if **Christ is in you**, although the body is dead because of sin, the Spirit is life because of righteousness."* (Rom 8:10 ESV). To the Corinthians, *"Examine yourselves, to see whether you are in the faith. Test yourselves. Or do you not realize this about yourselves, that **Jesus Christ is in you**?—unless indeed you fail to meet the test!"* (2 Cor 13:5 ESV). Think about that beautiful passage in Galatians, *"I have been crucified with Christ. It is no longer I who live, but **Christ who lives in me**. And the life I now live in the flesh I live by faith in the Son of God, who loved me and gave himself for me."* (Gal 2:20 ESV).

Jesus also revealed to his disciples before he left with them for the garden of Gethsemane that he would not leave them as orphans but that he would come to them. He reassured them with these words and reiterated the close relationship he would continue to have with them. (John 14:18-20 ESV).

One writer has said regarding all of these Scriptural passages that talk in one way or another about abiding in, dwelling in, or living in: "Let me say in the plainest, simplest, strongest way I can, that the dwelling of Christ in the believing heart is to be regarded as **plain, literal fact**—it is not to be weakened down into any idea of participation in his likeness, following his example or the like. A dead Plato may so influence his followers, but that is not how a living Christ influences his disciples."

Summary

We have looked at our risen Lord Jesus as a **saving** Lord Jesus, feeling his overwhelming love for his Father and for us. We have accepted that love with repentance, baptism, and commitment.

We have looked at our risen Lord Jesus as a **living** Lord Jesus, who can fill us with that zoe life and love that *"comes from God, "who "sent His only begotten Son into the world, that we might live (zoe) through him."*

We looked at the highest level of a personal relationship that can be attained when we saw the risen Lord Jesus as an **indwelling** Lord Jesus. An indwelling Lord Jesus is about a life where we *"will be made complete with all the fullness of life and power that comes from God."* Jesus tells us *"I am the vine; you are the branches. Whoever abides in me and I in him, he it is that bears much fruit, for apart from me you can do nothing."* (John 15:5 ESV). Through our relationship with our Lord Jesus, we rejoice in the *"fulness of life and power that comes from God."*

Paul writes to these new believers the following encouraging passage,

No, in all these things we are more than conquerors through him who loved us. For I am sure that neither death nor life, nor angels nor rulers, nor things present nor things to come, nor powers, nor height nor depth, nor anything else in all creation, will be able to separate us from the love of God in Christ Jesus our Lord (Rom 8:37-39 ESV).

Through our Lord, we have an overwhelming victory!

Russ Brierly
Moorestown Ecclesia, NJ

THE TIME OF SINGING HAS COME

A look at the Stories Behind the Songs, with Juliana Anderson

By Jessica Gelineau

LEVI Gelineau conducted the following interview for WCF's podcast, *"A Little Faith."* In it, Sis. Juliana K. Anderson, a lifelong lover of music and prolific composer of spiritual music, shares the stories behind some of her original songs that have now been compiled to form an easily accessible album. Whether these songs are old favorites or you have not yet encountered them, I think you'll be thankful for this collection.

Levi: We will talk about an upcoming music release you are putting out on Spotify and other streaming channels with WCF (Williamsburg Christadelphian Foundation). The name is *The Time of Singing Has Come.* What inspired this release?

Julie: I was at the Great Lakes Bible School last summer, my second time attending. My son Bro. Grant, who has attended several times, wanted to go, so I took him. I was asked to do the children's and the adult music that year, which I was very excited about. I used a lot of my own music. After hearing about the final programs, Bro. Paul Elliott and Bro. Mark Drabenstott asked if I would be interested in getting my music out there and suggested that WCF could help.

Levi: I'm really happy that you've gone through with this project. It was fun for me to listen to these songs. These are all recordings from other times, right?

Julie: Yes. We thought we could get it up and running faster that way, so I got permission from all the people who originally made the CDs to put an album together of my already pre-recorded songs. LORD willing, going forward, we are going to work on getting some other more recent songs done in a professional way.

Levi: Music has been important to you for a long time. Do you have a number of how many songs you've written?

Julie: My daughters and I made a list because we're going to try to make a book of all the music put together so that I don't have to look under the piano or in a box! We counted about 120 songs, between children's and adult songs. A lot more than I thought when we put them all together!

Levi: Let's talk about the songs on the album!

The Time of *Singing* Has Come

Songs of Encouragement and Exhortation

Compilation Album
Recordings from 1990 - 2007

By Juliana K. Anderson
Featuring Grant Anderson

The cover art for Juliana's compilation album, which was released through WCF Music in April 2023. Look for this image wherever you stream music!

Julie: I am going to go in order of the year I wrote them rather than the order on the album. "Hannah's Song," I wrote in 1990. The lyrics come from 1 Samuel 2, where we read Hannah's prayer after she gives her son Samuel to Eli. Hannah is my daughter's name, so you can tell I really liked the story of Hannah. Interestingly, Mary repeats a lot of the words of Hannah. When you think about it, it appears that Hannah was praying for a son, for the Messiah. In this particular song, she's rejoicing because God lifts up those who are low, and Mary says the same words. They were both looking for a Messiah.

The next set of songs on this album are from 1992. I wrote a cantata called "The Greatest of These is Love," that I used at Shippensburg Bible School and at what was Hanover Bible School at the time. The song "Love is Patient" is from 1 Corinthians 13. Everybody knows these verses are very well-loved because they're about love! God provided me with music when I read those verses, so I wrote that one. It's beautiful because it shows how love is an action. Love is something that we do. The other is "Let Yours Not Be the Outward Adorning," which talks about how it's not what we put on or what we have on the outside that matters. It's what comes out of the inside of your heart. Through Christ and through training our hearts, we can have the qualities of love.

"Let Yours Not Be the Outward Adorning" was put on the *Thy Kingdom Come* CD by the South Australia Christadelphian Youth Choir. And "Love is Patient" was on the Our Blessed Hope CD from South Australia. I know people don't use CDs so much anymore, but for those of us who remember them, they were used quite a bit.

Levi: When I listened to the music before this interview, I remembered "Love is Patient" because my mom would play Our Blessed Hope a bunch. I would have been a kid in the mid-nineties. I've heard that song many times, and I immediately recognized that one when I listened to the album.

Julie: Aww! That's really nice. Yeah, I was very excited when these got recorded. There's a special feeling when you've put notes together, and you can hear how they're supposed to sound in

Julie (Right) singing in a praise program with her daughter, Cassie Giordano.

your head. But until the voices come in and sing them, you really don't know what they're going to sound like. It's great to hear the song come alive with many voices. We played all these CDs for my kids too. I think my older kids are about your age.

The next group of songs are from the year 1994. The theme for the Bible Schools I was doing that summer was "May His Glory Fill the Whole Earth." One of the songs is called "Lift Up Your Eyes," and it's from Genesis 13. I wanted verses that talked about the land being inherited, that the reward will be on earth, and that God's earth will be filled with His glory. So I used Genesis 13:14-17, which is when Abraham is promised the land. *"Lift up your eyes and look from the place where you are northward and southward, eastward and westward. For all the land that you see, I will give to you and to your seed forever."* Musically, I was really excited about this song because it has a little bit of a Jewish sound to it, and a marching, upbeat style. When we take on the name of Christ, we become the seed of Abraham and march to the Kingdom with him.

Also from 1994 are the songs "The Time of Singing Has Come," which is what we named the album after, and "Behold, He's Coming Soon."

"The Time of Singing Has Come" is actually on this new album twice. The recording on the Shalom CD from British Columbia has a gorgeous male solo voice, and then the choir comes in. It's just a beautiful rendition of the song. The other song recording on the *One Faith, One Hope* CD from South Australia has the men come in first, the ladies come in, and the entire choir sings together. And that version has a descant, which I wrote later, and it just lends a different sound to the whole song. They're both very good, which shows me that when we can all sing together, we can be singing the same song, but we can do it differently. It doesn't mean that we're not at one with each other. It just means we each have a different voice, and all our voices being put together is important and special. So, I really enjoyed having the two different versions of that song.

"Behold, He's Coming Soon" is from Revelation 22. It was written in the program "May His Glory Fill the Whole Earth" and later recorded on the *Thy Kingdom Come* CD. It fits well with that theme because it talks about Christ coming back to the earth. I had a lot more trouble with this one because, most of the time, when I write a song, I read the Scripture, and then the song comes to me. That time, I had a melody that I really liked, and I was trying and praying to get verses that would fit it. It took me a little while, but

I finally came up with, "Behold, He's coming soon. He will bring his reward to repay everyone for what he has done. He is the Alpha and the Omega, He is the first and the last, the beginning and end."

That song changes keys as you go up, and the piano has these rolling swells; the sound is quite different from the other songs.

Then the final song that I haven't yet talked about on the new album is quite emotional. I think you, Levi, will remember the story behind this, "A Prayer of Moses." It was composed in 2007, and this recording is from the Manitoulin Youth Choir singing it. When I first wrote this song, I was at the piano at home in my music room and I had the words and melody. "Satisfy in the morning with your steadfast love, that you may rejoice and be glad. Be glad all your days, make us glad as many days as thou afflicted us, and as many years as evil you have

Julie singing with her son, Grant Anderson.

seen, or we have seen." I really didn't know how much that would affect me, and how much I would sing that song, and how much I needed that song until a little bit later, which I'll share with you in a moment.

My son Grant, who was 20 years old at the time, came into the room, he heard this, and he was so excited. And he said, "Mom, that sounds like a spiritual! I want to arrange that." Little did I know, but the Manitoulin Youth Conference was doing Moses that summer. And this song is from Psalms 91 and 92, which is the song of Moses. Grant was working for a music director at a high school near us who had him put in all the keyboards and all the computer systems into a music lab there, fairly new at the time, for students to be able to write and do different things with music. So, Grant took what I had written to that lab. He made a beautiful arrangement, then he called me and said, "Mom, you have to come and listen." He took me there around 11 PM. I listened with tears. It was beautiful. I was so, so excited. So was Grant!

"A Prayer of Moses" was put into the music program for the Youth Conference that year. But, as I said, little did we know what was coming. Grant couldn't make it to the Friday night concert at Manitoulin that year because he had previous commitments, so he left the camp early. He got in a car accident on the way home and went into a coma. In fact, he was in a coma for about six weeks. During this time, the young people at the camp had to decide whether they would sing the song because it was so emotional and because Grant and I had written it. And they decided to go ahead and sing it. The recording that we have on the new album is from that performance. Some of the young people sang it again when they came to the Detroit hospital Grant was moved to.

Levi: Yes, I remember very well how emotional that time was at the camp, being there then. My wife, Sis. Jess and I were there at the camp, and Jess was performing in the choir. So her voice is in there somewhere. And performing that, knowing what we all knew, was a very emotional moment because, for so long, we didn't know how it was going to work out with Grant.

Julie: Yeah, we didn't know.

Levi: For such a long time. So, I'm glad we're highlighting that and sharing that song again.

Julie: And we were very glad the camp sang it because we played it several times for Grant afterward, and, as I said, they sang it at the hospital. He didn't get to hear it from his hospital room, but we heard it as a family, and it meant so much to us to know the support that we had and how the music and Grant touched people. So we are very grateful and thankful that it can be shared on this album.

Levi: Thank you. It's amazing to have all those stories, and it really is a collection, right? Recordings from 1990 to 2007. Seven songs. Multiple countries, multiple choirs, all together. Definitely, very cool.

Julie: I wanted to add one more story, something else to show how much music works in the brain and how wonderful it is, and one of the reasons why God tells us to sing. Grant, when he first started waking up from the coma, could not remember writing this song, but he could remember the song, and he could remember all the words. Praise God, he was able to have his memory come back later. It took almost a year to get his memory back for many of the events that happened before his accident, but the words and the music were there in his heart and mind the whole time. It's quite amazing.

Levi: That is absolutely stunning. There's a mysterious, obviously spiritual thing around music. It has such power. Thank you so much for your time, Julie, and for sharing so much. I'm excited for more people to benefit from the album.

Julie: Yes, thank you. It's been a pleasure. Music has been a big part of my life since I was young. I didn't go into music because my father said it wasn't very reliable as a source of income, but God is using me with music in a different way. And I'm very grateful.

Levi: I'm thankful that God has and is using your music to help so many other people. Thank you!

Jessica Gelineau,
Simi Hills Ecclesia, CA

If you liked this article, you may be interested in reading or revisiting Sis. Julie's article that was published in the January 2021 Tidings Magazine, titled "In Harmony". www.tidings. org/articles/in-harmony.

Listen to *The Time of Singing Has Come: Songs of Encouragement and Exhortation* on Spotify, YouTube, or any other major streaming platform under WCF Christadelphian Music.

The episode of the WCF podcast "A Little Faith" that this interview appears on was released on April 19, 2023.

Songs for God's Children

Digital Music Book

It is exciting to share that the "Songs for God's Children" digital music book is now available as a companion to the album! The book contains lead sheets for piano, guitar chords, hand motions, and suggested activities for kids that pair well with the songs. This resource is designed for use in Sunday Schools, children's Bible School music programs, or even within homes. Please take a look and see how you can use it, and share it with a Sunday School teacher, friend, or family member today!

The book can be freely downloaded at **wcfoundation.org/wcf-music**

PART 3

WORDS I HO
I NEVER HE
AGAIN

By David Levin

*Christadelphian Cliches, Misqu
Pat Phrases, Wrested Scriptures,
Legalistic Formulas*

"Five is the number of grace"

OFTEN repeated but never verified, "Five is the number of grace" (hereafter 5 = grace) is the poster child for Christadelphian phrases that need to be deep-sixed. Or deep-fived.

What's wrong with it? Everything. Five isn't the number of grace because grace doesn't have a number; if it did, it surely wouldn't be five. If five is the number of anything, it's something unsavory.

What's at stake? Not much theologically—no essential doctrine hangs on associating the number five with grace. What is at stake is our community's integrity as Bible students and critical thinkers.

How to improve it? Can't be fixed. Needs to be expunged. Five isn't the number of anything, and grace doesn't have another number to flee to.

Five isn't the number of grace because grace doesn't have a number; if it did, it surely wouldn't be five...

Discussion: Of the scores of times I've heard this assertion, I've never heard a gram of evidence to support it. It's invariably made when there happens to be either the number five or a group of five nice words or ideas (as arbitrary as the included text size might be), and the speaker or a participant in the Bible class informs us, "Five is the number of grace."

Grace has five letters in either English or Greek—that's about how cogent most of these observations are.

Where did it come from?

As far as I can tell, the origin of "five is the number of grace" traces to the prolific 19th-century Bible linguist and scholar E.W. Bullinger. He has a brief account of the representational meaning of numbers in Appendix 6 of the *Companion Bible* and a full account in his book, *Number in Scripture*. The chapter on "Five" is pathetically weak, but that didn't seem to hinder its spread as gospel.

Bullinger's support for 5 = grace is "4+1=5." That's clear proof of the thesis because Bullinger explains that "4" represents physical creation, and one is the activity of God. God acting on the natural creation is grace. Slam dunk. 5 = grace.

Why didn't he opt for 2+3? Maybe something in his scheme wouldn't click? Likewise, 6-1= 5, but how would you get grace out of that equation? The number of humanity minus the activity of God equals five, which is God's grace. You can see that I'm jabbing at the arbitrariness of the original calculus.

Criteria for Assigning an Equivalency

Before deconstructing 5 = grace, we need to back up and establish criteria for making any statement of the form *S* (the symbol) in some way represents or indicates *Z* (the symbolized), where *S* is some identifiable entity, such as the number, color, animal, or body part. And *Z* is some concept, such as grace, priesthood, wealth, resurrection, or death.

To assert that any *S* symbolizes *Z*, the following criteria must be met:

1. Both *S* and *Z* must be identifiable, discrete entities.

2. *S* appears only in the context of *Z*; *S* never appears in the context of *X, Y,* or anything else.

3. No other entity symbolizes *Z* unless the same criteria can be established for two or more symbols.

4. At least some associations of *Z* with *S* are explicit; others can be inferred.

Let's first look at a hypothetical example: something other than 5 = grace: purple is the color of royalty. This assertion has the same form as 5 = grace, so the same rules apply.

For purple to be the color of royalty, it must meet these criteria:

1. Purple and royalty are discrete and identifiable entities

2. Whenever purple appears, it is in the context of royalty. Purple never appears associated with any class other than royalty.

3. No other color appears in the context of royalty.

4. At least some associations of purple are explicitly associated with royalty.

As for #1, purple and royalty are discrete and identifiable, so we're good there. Secondly, the test of purple = royalty requires that purple always and only appears in the context of royalty; purple is never associated with peasants or warriors, and (#4) in at least some of the contexts where purple appears, the mention of royalty is explicit. For instance, if the association is established with explicit occurrences, and elsewhere you read "Abniezer sat in his purple chair," you understand that the text is implying that Abniezer has some connection to royalty—maybe he's an estranged heir to the throne or a usurper.

Criterion #3, no other color being associated with royalty, demands some slack. The queen could have crimson trim on her purple robe or white bloomers under her purple gown. Several kings with yellow robes, however, would pose a threat to the hypothesis. Note that while it is necessary for purple to always appear in the context of royalty, the hypothesis purple = royalty does not require that every mention of royalty has a reference to purple.

These four association rules make it difficult to say whether any given *S* represents or indicates *Z*. The association needs to be tight and unique if it is to have any expositional value. However, we're not dealing with mathematical equations or logical syllogisms. Given that the Bible was written over millennia, in at least three languages, and covers many cultures, it's okay to relax the above criteria. Still, to make an assertion about Bible symbology, you better have some pretty tight evidence and solid explanations for nonconforming data. If "five" repeatedly occurs with other items, such as death or taxes, its meaning is unreliable.

Does 5 = grace meet these criteria?

The number five is indeed discrete and identifiable. A grouping of five related items or five occurrences of a word could be disputed, however, on the grounds that the size of the text is arbitrarily assigned to include five and only five of the items. Romans 5:15-21 (NIV) is a good example. The word "grace" appears five times in this well-known passage, contrasting the consequences of Adam's sin and Jesus' atoning sacrifice. The length of the passage is arbitrary, though; it could end at v. 19, or it could also include the first verse of Romans 6—there being, of course, no verses or chapter divisions in Paul's writing.

Also of note is if you do keep 5:15-21 as the natural boundaries of Paul's thought (to make sure you have five occurrences of "grace"), you are also demarking five occurrences of the word "sin."

Is "grace" a discrete, identifiable concept? Couldn't be further away. Almost any circumstance can be described as an act of God's grace if you want to derive 5 = grace from that passage. David's five stones are clearly about warfare, but it's easy to slide in an amorphous version of grace here—God showed grace to David by providing five smooth stones."

How about this one: *"Are not five sparrows sold for two pennies?"* (Luke 12:6 NIV). If grace can be read into this passage (e.g., God's grace is shown by valuing us more than the sparrows), then five is the number of anything, and something that means anything means nothing.

Is Five Associated with Something Else?

Moving on to criterion #2, are there any instances where the number five, or some group of five, clearly indicates something other than "grace?" Can it be demonstrated that "five" is not uniquely associated with "grace?"

How about the five books of the law? Five cities of the Philistines? Two deal breakers right there.

The following list absolutely dispels 5 = grace.

- Five persons specifically mentioned die on Gilboa: Saul, his three sons, and his armor bearer (1 Sam 31:6).

- Five Amorite kings fight Joshua; "five kings" is repeated five times (Josh 10:5, 16, 17, 22, 23); they are hanged on five trees (v. 26).

- Five kings rebel against Chedorlaomer and his allies (Gen 14:2-9).

- David selects five stones to fight Goliath (I Sam 17:40).

- Five giant Philistine warriors, Goliath, and four more are listed in 2 Sam 21:18-22.

- Five Philistine cities with five lords who get five golden mice and five golden tumors (I Sam 6:16-18).

- David utters a five-fold curse on Joab for slaying Abner (2 Sam 3:29).

- The Hebrew idiom for an armed sortie is to go out "by fives" (Josh

> Our beliefs are founded on abundant evidence, reasonableness, and aptness. Uncritical adherence to 5 = grace ... reflects poorly on our highly valued principle of accurate Biblical investigation.

1:14, 4:13; Jdgs 7:11, and possibly also Exod 13:18). This idiom may or may not be footnoted in your Bible version, but it's evident in Hebrew.

The above examples are all associated with war and fighting and couldn't be further from God's grace. Five does not appear to be uniquely associated with warfare, but it does show up many times in that context.

In another vein, and without doubt another nail in the coffin for "5 = grace" is I Sam 2:21. After Hannah (which translates to "grace") bore Samuel, she was blessed with five more children—three boys and two girls. That makes six children total. And if it is the case that the five includes Samuel (the context leans toward the five are in addition), then that's precisely also the offspring of Saul: three boys and two girls (I Sam 14:49). You can't say God was gracious to Hannah and not include Saul.

Criteria #3 and 4 are now superfluous to dismiss 5 = grace. Even if you can find a few groups of five somethings that seem pretty closely allied to a standard definition of grace, that doesn't help unless you want to assert that "five is sometimes associated with one conception of grace." That's hardly useful.

The formulaic 5 = grace has no validity, and it is an embarrassment to keep hearing it asserted. We are a body of believers who take Bible study seriously. Our beliefs are founded on abundant evidence, reasonableness, and aptness. Uncritical adherence to 5 = grace, even if it's a relatively minor doctrinal point, reflects poorly on our highly valued principle of accurate Biblical investigation.

A Big Problem About the Word Grace

Do you know where zero = grace? That's the number of times the word "grace" appears in our Statement of Faith (BASF). No mention of the word or the concept of salvation by grace. Now, that's a serious concern.

David Levin,
Denver Ecclesia, CO

GETTING TO KNOW OUR GOD AND JESUS

PART 2

By Jim Styles

God's Election of His Family (Rom 9)

WE grew up thinking, like the Jews did in the Bible that we were the only people God could save because we were the good soil, and the rest of the world was not. This is an area that, over time, we have had to modify and correct our understanding. As parents, we thought that if we raised our children by doing the Bible readings at home and taking them to CYC, Sunday School, and memorial meeting, we were guaranteed they would love the Truth, get baptized, and be accepted into the family of God. This thought was also a misconception!

This article is not about who will be accepted at the judgment seat of Christ but who can join God's family and may be responsible at the Judgment Seat.

There are over eight billion people on Earth today. Does everyone get the same opportunity to join God's family? There are only around 60,000 Christadelphians alive today. Most of the humans who have lived on earth since the time of Adam never knew about the gospel of God. Were all those people who never knew the gospel bad soil who could never understand the gospel? We don't think so anymore.

Before reading Romans 9, we should read Romans 1, where Paul develops Gentiles' failure to attain God's righteousness. In Romans 2, he points out that Jews were even worse because of all the privileges God gave them, and they still did not attain God's righteousness. Then, in Romans 3, Paul concludes everyone has sinned and fallen short of God's glory, so God intervened and justified His family by His grace, through faith, just as He had always planned. In Romans 4, Paul reminds us that "Abraham believed [had faith in] God, and it was counted to him as righteousness." And finally, in Romans 5, he lays out how God loves His children and always intends to save them by giving them His free gift of grace.

It becomes clear that we would have no hope if God had not intervened in our lives. No one would be saved. Years ago, we used to tell our interested friends that if they would only read the Bible for themselves, with an open mind, they would find the Truth. But it turns out that is not true. Many of them did read their Bibles and knew them very well, maybe better than some of us! But they still did not see God's truth.

When Paul wrote Romans 9, he understood God's election of His family, which was developed from personal experience and inspiration. Paul had spent years studying the Bible, researching, and yet still persecuting the true believers of Jesus Christ until Jesus opened his eyes! Paul understood from personal experience that it is not about how much effort we put in to find God ourselves or help others to be saved, but rather, it is all about the mercy and grace God chooses to give freely. No wonder Paul reminded the Ephesians that it was all about what God chooses to do in their lives:

That the God of our Lord Jesus Christ, the Father of glory, may give you a spirit of wisdom and of revelation in the knowledge of him, having the eyes of your hearts enlightened, that you may know what is the hope to which he has called you, what are the riches of his glorious inheritance in the saints. (Eph 1:17-18). [1]

That's not to say that we don't have to read and pray, but it is a reality check that no matter how much we read and pray, it is up to God to enlighten the eyes of our hearts. Without God's intervention and revelation in His merciful kindness to let us understand, all our efforts are in vain. When Jesus returns, he will convert billions of humans alive today, the same people we couldn't convert no matter how much we preached to them. We might think they are not good soil today, but Jesus will finally allow them to understand the gospel when he opens their eyes, like he did for Paul. The parable of the Sower is all about how people receive the gospel. Many people today will not **receive** the gospel, but when Jesus returns and opens their eyes, they will finally embrace the gospel of God. This idea changes the way we preach today. We don't need to hammer the Truth into people. God wants us to present the gospel to them using our Bibles and demonstrating our way of life, patterned after the life of Christ. At the same time, we pray God will open their eyes to understand because it is up to Him to enlighten those He invites into His family—not us! Remember when the disciples asked Jesus why he spoke in parables? His reply was:

To you it has been given to know the secrets of the kingdom of heaven, but to them it has not been given...This is why I speak to them in parables, because seeing they do not see, and hearing they do not hear, nor do they understand. (Matt 13:11, 13).

He clearly told his disciples:

No one can come to me unless the Father who sent me draws him. But there are some of you who do not believe..." (For Jesus knew from the beginning who those were who did not believe, and who it was who would betray him.) And he said, *"This is why I told you that no one can come to me unless it is granted him by the Father."* (John 6:44, 64-65).

No wonder it says of Lydia that *"the Lord opened her heart to respond to the things spoken by Paul."* (Acts 16:14-15 NASB).

The best Bible exposition on God's election of His family is in Romans 9. Paul sets out to explain to Jews that God chose to work almost exclusively with Abraham and his children for about 2,000 years. But since the death of Jesus, the gospel has been spreading among the Gentiles. He develops the theme that this is God's family, and God can choose whoever He wants to invite and enlighten for His family. It's not up to us. God designed it so no flesh will glory in His presence.

In verses 1-5, Paul had great sorrow and continual grief in his heart for his Jewish countrymen. They had been given so many privileges, but they would not believe and crucified God's Son.

In verses 6-8, Paul points out God's plan had not failed because God never intended to save every Israelite. God only invited and enlightened Isaac, not Ishmael. Abraham and Sarah devised a plan according to the flesh to have a child, Ishmael, but God did not invite Ishmael because he was a child of the flesh, not according to the promise of God. Abraham had pleaded with God, *"Oh that Ishmael might live before you!"* (Gen 17:18) because Abraham loved Ishmael and raised him for about fourteen years and taught him about Yahweh, his God. But God wanted to make it clear to all Abraham's descendants that God's family was based on God's choice and God's mercy, not how hard humans work or what they want. So Abraham accepted God's decision, sent Hagar away, and disowned Ishmael. A few years later, God told Abraham to take his **only son** Isaac, whom he loved, when testing his faith.

Paul revealed that God knew that many Jews would think He rejected Ishmael because he was the child of a slave woman, so in the next generation, God made it absolutely clear. Here's Paul's explanation:

> Not only that, but Rebekah's children had one and the same father, our father Isaac. Yet, before the twins were born or had done anything good or bad—**in order that God's purpose in election might stand: not by works but by him who calls**—she was told, "The older will serve the younger." Just as it is written: "Jacob I loved, but Esau I hated." (Rom 9:10-13 NIV).

You can't miss the point! Rebekah had been barren for over twenty years, and then God caused her to conceive. Then, from two twins of the same dad and mom, God chose one and not the other before they were born or had any opportunity to do good or evil. God wanted the issue perfectly clear to all Abraham's descendants that their privileged position was because of what God did for them, not any works they would do. It's all about God's family, who God calls or elects, and His merciful kindness to train people to live by faith so they will reveal God's eternal life and His eternal way of life.

You may be thinking God made this choice because, in His foreknowledge, he knew what kind of people Jacob and Esau would become. But you missed Paul's point. Paul mentions nothing about God's foreknowledge but instead bases his exposition on God's choice before the children were born and had done anything! In Romans 1-2, Paul made it clear that no one would be saved without God's intervention. Jacob was not a better person than Esau by birth. God records in the Bible that Jacob was a schemer, trying to accomplish his will through deceit. But God intervened in Jacob's life and trained him to become a very different person—one of God's children. Genesis records the painful experiences God brought into Jacob's life, as angels disciplined him and changed him into a new man, predestined to be conformed to the image of Jesus Christ. God did not do this for Esau. This situation shows the difference God's election makes in our lives. As Paul puts it in Romans 9:21, "Has the potter no right over the clay, to make **out of the same lump** one vessel for honored use and another for dishonorable use?" Notice it is out of the same lump of clay. Not one out of good clay and the other out of bad clay!

It's interesting to note that the brethren who amended clause 24 of the BASF worded the addition as "the responsible (namely, those who know the revealed will of God, **and have been called upon to submit to it**)" because they realized responsibility is not just about knowing, but also must include God's calling. We can teach children and adults today about the revealed will of God, but if God does not call them, they are not responsible at the Judgment Seat of Christ. That may be hard to swallow and accept for many parents, but it is solid Bible teaching from God's perspective, not ours. This notion brings peace to many parents who have tried and tried to enlighten some of their children, like Abraham did with Ishmael and Isaac with Esau, only to find their children walk away. It's God's family, so He chooses and calls who He wants to include, not us. So we learn to pray and pray that God will choose to call our spouse, parents, children, grandchildren, or friends and not depend so much on our efforts to convert them. We do our part, but God does the calling and enlightens the minds. As Psalm 127 reminds us, "Unless the Lord builds the house, those who build it labor in vain. Unless the Lord watches over the city, the watchman stays awake in vain." Notice how the rest of the Psalm reminds us that we don't have to do it all ourselves and then leads on to children being "a heritage of the LORD."

In Romans 9:14-18, Paul anticipates the Jew's thinking that God is not fair to choose some and not others. This thinking is humanistic! From God's perspective, no one deserves to be saved, and it is only in His mercy and grace that anyone will be granted to enter His family forever. Paul reminds them that God said to Moses, "'I will have mercy on whom I have mercy, and I will have compassion on whom I will have compassion.' So it depends not on human will or exertion, but on God who has mercy."

In Romans 8:30, Paul had already explained how God deals with mankind today. Of all the people alive today, some of them could be good soil. Of those, God predestined some to be called and enlightened. Some of those called respond by their own free will, and God justifies them. And some of those justified remain faithful to the end, and God will glorify them. That's how Paul explained God's calling and election.

The implications of this topic for our families and friends are that we must continuously pray that God, in His kindness and mercy, will call them into His family. We must do everything we can to teach them God's ways, but we also need to realize that it's God's choice to call them or not. We don't have to beat the Truth into them and can't choose who God will call. Then, if they do decide to follow God's ways, we have to thank God for his mercy and appreciate that He has done what we could never do—enlighten the eyes of their understanding. And if they don't respond right now, don't ever give up and don't live in the guilt that it's your fault! God may wait until a later time to enlighten them. Hopefully, this will bring some peace and trust to you as you raise children and grandchildren and share the gospel with your friends and neighbors.

God has graciously allowed you to understand the gospel of God. Don't waste your opportunity! Billions of people today have not been given this privilege, but you have. Embrace it, appreciate it, and thank God every day for allowing you to understand. Then pray God will include your families, ecclesias, and friends in His election. Always remember that it's God's family, not ours. So, try to understand and cooperate with God's choices today to invite people and train them to join His immortal family of angels. "Thanks be to God for His inexpressible gift!" (2 Cor 9:15).

Sue and Jim Styles,
Simi Hills Ecclesia, CA

1 All Scriptural citations are taken from the English Standard Version, unless specifically noted.

PREACHING THE
FIRST PRINCIPLES
IN A
POST-CHRISTIAN
WORLD
PART 2

By Richard Morgan

THE Apostle Paul's second missionary journey found him preaching for the first time in the predominantly Gentile world of darkness. His route took him through Philippi, Thessalonica and Berea until he ended up in Athens, a city famous for classical philosophy, including men like Socrates, who lived there his whole life a few hundred years before Paul. Despite having lost its luster of previous years, Athens was still considered in Paul's day a center of learning, alongside his home city of Tarsus and Alexandria in Egypt.

Luke records, *"While Paul was waiting for them at Athens, his spirit was provoked within him as he saw that the city was full of idols."* (Acts 17:16).[1] The phrase *"full of idols"* is one word in Greek, *katedidoios*, carrying with it the idea that Athens was like a forest of idolatry. Roman satirist Petronius, a contemporary of Paul, wrote concerning Athens, "It is easier to meet a god in the street than a human."

Perhaps Paul's mind went to these words from Isaiah, *"Their land is filled with idols; they bow down to the work of their hands, to what their own fingers have made."* (Isa 2:8). However, there's another clear echo with Deuteronomy 32, the passage we looked at in last month's article. There, we're told God's reaction to idolatry that *"stirred him to jealousy with strange gods"* (v16) and *"they have provoked me to anger with their idols"* (v. 21). In other words, Paul felt how God felt when he looked at the forest of idols.

Isaiah also talks about provocation. *"A people who provoke me to my face continually, sacrificing in gardens and making offerings on bricks"* (Isa. 65:3), a passage which hints at the gospel going to the Gentiles in the first verse:

I was ready to be sought by those who did not ask for me; I was ready to be found by those who did not seek me. I said, "Here I am, here I am," to a nation that was not called by my name. (Isa 65:1).

Indeed, Paul himself quoted this verse in Romans 10 in a passage where he contrasts Jewish and Gentile responses to the gospel message. In Romans 10, he quotes from that passage in Deuteronomy we just looked at, *"I will make you jealous of those who are not a nation; with a foolish nation I will make you angry."* (Rom 10:19). Then he quotes the verse from Isaiah, *"I have been found by those who did not seek me; I have shown myself to those who did not ask for me."* (Rom 10:20), speaking of the Gentiles.

We saw last month how Paul experienced the different reactions from Jews and Gentiles to his preaching. In Pisidian Antioch, the Jews rejected the message, so he turned to the Gentiles (Acts 13:44-47). The Jews were guilty of idolatry in the sense of their dependence on cultic ritualism. However, when preaching to the Gentiles, he found people willing to leave their cultic rituals and turn to the one true and living God. We can experience the same thing. Preaching to fellow Christians about the one true God can be difficult, but when we turn to the "Gentiles" of the world around us, we can succeed if we follow Paul's example in Athens.

Note again, those words from Isaiah 65:1 quoted in Romans 10:20, *"I was ready to be found by those who did not seek me."* The Gentiles had no reason to seek Yahweh, God of Israel. Still, during his speech in Athens, Paul told them *"that they should seek God, and perhaps feel their way toward him and find him."* (Acts 17:27). Likewise, the people in the world around us see no reason to seek God. Still, we have the tools to be able to preach about the one true God so that they might end up seeking after him and finding him.

Having been provoked by the forest of idols in Athens, what did Paul do? Luke records, *"So he reasoned in the synagogue with the Jews and the devout persons, and in the marketplace every day with those who happened to be there."* (Acts 17:17). Paul encountered three types of people: Jews, people steeped in superstitious religion (the devout persons), and those he encountered in the marketplace—the Agora— which was a marketplace of philosophical ideas. We know some of those more specifically because, in the next verse, we're told that among them were "Epicurean and Stoic philosophers." We, too, will meet a mix of people when preaching— Christians, people devoted to various superstitions, and the equivalent of Epicureans and Stoics.

The word *"reasoned"* in verse 17 in Greek is dialoegomai, which contains the idea of having a dialog within it. In other words, Paul had a conversation with the people he met. He wasn't just standing up and delivering a talk. This style is interesting because Athens had been the home of Socrates, one of the most famous Greek philosophers. Socrates' favorite teaching method was called the Elenchus technique, or the Socratic Method, often described using *dialoegomai*. Socrates employed his technique in a dialog, asking many questions about a particular concept. The aim of this back-and-forth dialog was to wake people out of their dogmatism into genuine intellectual curiosity.

While Acts 17 contains a speech by the Apostle Paul, it was also the result of him using the Elenchus technique that he reached the hearts and minds of his listeners. It's a great lesson for us when we try to preach first principle doctrines. It is one thing to tell people the Truth as we understand it simply, but a far better way is to ask questions–to get people to really think about important matters.

Luke presents Paul as a Socrates redivivus (revived). Socrates spent his whole time in Athens and used to converse with sophists and philosophers, as Paul does in the marketplace, using the Elenchus technique. But there's one other connection between the two men. Socrates was executed after he was charged with introducing foreign deities to Athens. Paul is charged with the same thing. *"Some of the Epicurean and Stoic philosophers also conversed with him. And some said, 'What does*

> It is one thing to tell people the Truth as we understand it simply, but a far better way is to ask questions– to get people to really think about important matters.

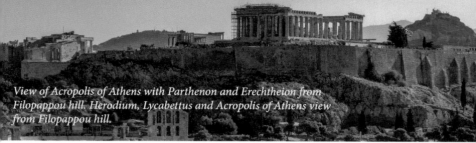

View of Acropolis of Athens with Parthenon and Erechtheion from Filopappou hill. Herodium, Lycabettus and Acropolis of Athens view from Filopappou hill.

this babbler wish to say?' Others said, 'He seems to be a preacher of foreign divinities'—because he was preaching Jesus and the resurrection." (v. 18). Verse 19 then records that *"they took him and brought him to the Areopagus,"* which probably means he was arrested and brought before a tribunal to answer the charge against him, just as happened to Socrates.

In fact, the word for *"preacher,"* *katangeleus*, in verse 18, a hapax legomenon (a term only used once) in Scripture, is the same word used in the charge against Socrates.

Why does Luke paint the picture of Paul being a Socrates redivivus? In verse 18, they call him a *"babbler"* which literally means a "seed picker" or someone who scavenges. The idea behind the word is of someone philosophically untrained novice who spouts forth bits of street philosophy. However, Luke wants us to be assured that Paul is no such thing but instead is on a par with one of the greatest of all philosophers.

Sometimes, we can seem unsophisticated in this world of modern-day philosophical thinking. We believe and teach unfashionable and old Bible concepts like Jesus and the resurrection. It seems like a lot

of babble to those whose ideas align with more up-to-date philosophies like postmodernism, scientism, and relativism. But we have the answers to the big questions of life. Our task is to use the Elenchus technique by asking the right questions and bringing people to realize that the Bible is right after all.

Now, of all the sophisticated thinkers in Athens, it is significant that Luke singles out the Epicurean and Stoic philosophers. Remember, Paul will try to convince people to leave the idolatry and cultic ritualism of their pagan ideas and embrace the true and living God of the Bible. What is interesting about the Epicureans and Stoics is that, of the groups in Athens, these were the most critical of religious ritualism and idolatry. At least theoretically.

The highest goal in the life of the Epicureans was pleasure. Diogenes Laertius says it was "absence of pain in the body and trouble in the soul." (Vit. 10.131). They believed in the theory of Atomism–that everything, including the gods, was made up of atoms that were always in motion. Things form when atoms collide, something they call the "swerve." Since these collisions were entirely random, the Epicureans believed in the concept of free will. They did not have any belief in an afterlife. The soul did not survive death, and the atoms disintegrated into nothing. They did believe that gods existed, but they lived in a far-off realm of supreme pleasure and had no dealings with human beings. As a result, they had no fear of the supernatural and were not superstitious, meaning they were functional atheists.

The Stoics said that God was the divine Logos or Cosmic Reason. They were pantheists, meaning everything is God, and God is in everything. They believed humans have a divine spark, which returns to the divine Logos at death. According to the Stoics, the way to encounter God was by looking for him using reason. They lived by an austere moral code and said that to desire things such as wealth and reputation was irrational and the cause of misery. The only good humans can do is to control their own moral choices. Unlike the Epicureans, the Stoics believed that all events are predetermined, so there is no free will.

Perhaps you've met the modern-day equivalents of the Epicureans and Stoics? For instance, as functional atheists and believing in an ancient form of evolution, the Epicureans have a lot in common with the atheists and naturalists of today. These people deny all forms of supernaturalism. On the other hand, some live reasonable lives, trying to be good people, like the Stoics. In today's world, pantheism is seen in the appeal of Eastern religion and the idea that spirituality is found in nature rather than in a personal God.

What most of these people have in common is a rejection of organized religion, much like the Epicureans and Stoics of Paul's day. While organized religion is still extant in Western society (the equivalent to the first-century Jewish synagogue model), it is on the wane, and more and more people we meet fall into the Epicurean or Stoic mold. As we shall see in his speech, Paul could expertly weave into his argument an ability to find common ground with people who had no idea– or any initial interest—in the God of the Bible. He also appealed to those *"devout persons"* of verse 17, the main populous of Athens, who we see today in people who are devoutly religious or superstitious.

However, Paul's attempts to find common ground did not interfere with his direct preaching of the first principles of our faith. But he was misunderstood when he preached *"Jesus and the resurrection"* (v. 18). They thought he was teaching about new gods called "Jesus" and "Anastasis." The Athenians had no concept in their combined philosophies of physical resurrection of the day, so Paul's words sounded more like he was preaching about a goddess called Anastasis—the Greek word for resurrection but also a female name.

We, too, are going to say things that sound like gobbledygook to many people. But when people do accuse us of being babblers, and we're misunderstood, we can take our opportunity, as Paul does in his speech, and find a way to reach into the darkness and open some blind eyes.

Richard Morgan,
Simi Hills Ecclesia, CA

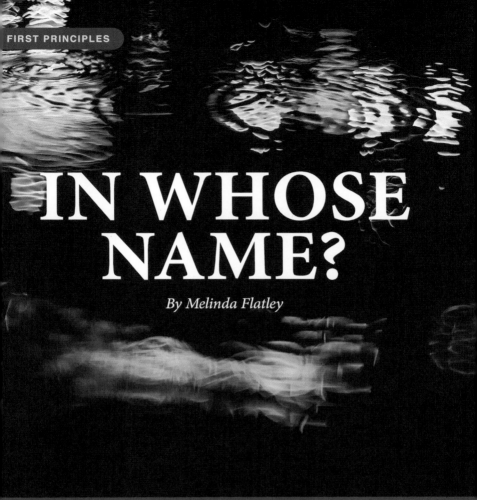

IN WHOSE NAME?

By Melinda Flatley

EVERY Christadelphian baptism I've attended, including mine, has ended with the pronouncement: "I baptize you in the name of the Father, and the Son and the Holy Spirit." For some time, I've been puzzled about why we use the Trinity formula at this most important occasion in a believer's life. After all, it's a doctrine we reject. Whenever I've posed this question to others, the answer has generally been along the lines of: "Well, it's in the Bible, and it was okay with Bro. Robert Roberts." And, indeed, it is. It's in *The Ecclesial Guide*[1] and here in what we call The Great Commission, given by Jesus to his disciples:

> *And Jesus came up and spoke to them, saying, "All authority has been given to Me in heaven and on earth. Go therefore and make disciples of all the nations, baptizing them in the name of the Father and the Son and the Holy Spirit, teaching them to observe all that I commanded you." (Matt 28:19).*[2]

WDJS—What Did Jesus Say?

But is this really what Jesus said? Is this wording consistent with other evidence we can turn to in Scripture? Did Jesus really instruct the disciples to teach and baptize in the Trinity? If so, they certainly disobeyed parts of this instruction. No instances in the New Testament describe a baptism in the name of a Triune God. But many passages describe how the early apostles baptized solely *"in the name of Jesus Christ."* Here is just a sample:

*Peter said to them, "Repent, and each of you be baptized **in the name of Jesus Christ** for the forgiveness of your sins; and you will receive the gift of the Holy Spirit."* (Acts 2:38).

*But when they believed Philip preaching the good news about the kingdom of God and **the name of Jesus Christ**, they were being baptized, men and women alike.* (Acts 8:12, 16).

*And he ordered them to be baptized **in the name of Jesus Christ**.* (Acts 10:48).

*When they heard this, they were baptized **in the name of the Lord Jesus**.* (Acts 19:5).

*For all of you who were baptized **into Christ** have clothed yourselves with Christ.* (Gal 3:27).

Moreover, the parallel accounts about The Great Commission contain no hint of baptism in the name of the Father, Son, and Holy Spirit.

And He said to them, "Go into all the world and preach the gospel to all creation. He who has believed and has been baptized shall be saved; but he who has disbelieved shall be condemned. These signs will accompany those who have believed: in My name they will cast out demons; they will speak with new tongues; they will pick up serpents, and if they drink any deadly poison, it will not hurt them; they will lay hands on the sick, and they will recover." (Mark 16:15-18).[3]

Repentance for forgiveness of sins should be proclaimed in His name to all the nations, beginning from Jerusalem. (Luke 24:47).

The one who believes in Him is not judged; the one who does not believe has been judged already, because he has not believed in the name of the only Son of God. (John 3:18).

A Mystery... a Forgery?

So, where do we turn for an explanation of this apparent contradiction? This situation has all the hallmarks of the convoluted scheme in Dan Brown's thriller, *The Da Vinci Code*. My research has taken me down an elaborate series of rabbit holes, beginning on a mountain in Galilee, where Jesus gave the Great Commission, and ending in Turkey, where a man sat in a position of honor on the dais beside Emperor Constantine at the Council of Nicaea. In between, we need to look at extra-Biblical accounts of and by early Church Fathers who lived and wrote in the first few centuries after Jesus rose from the dead and ascended to heaven.

How curious is it that not a single Greek manuscript from the first 300 years after Christ contains the last pages of the Gospel of Matthew nor the *"in his name"* wording? It's just not there, anywhere. Not only is the wording missing, but the entire last pages of every existing copy are missing. Not until manuscripts dated after AD 340 do we all of a sudden see the Matthew 28:19 wording currently in our Bibles regarding Trinitarian baptism. Was this a marginal note that somehow became incorporated in the text? Or was a deliberate fraud committed to suppress the original Great Commission and insert the threefold name as a later doctrinal expansion? If so, how could something so significant be accomplished without discovery?

Because no evidence has survived to preserve and support an older reading, we can't prove that someone or a group of someone's perpetrated a scam to protect the idea of the Trinity.

Or Can We?

Well, there may be a few firsthand witnesses we can consult—those early Church Fathers.

The first step in a search such as this is to investigate what scholars know about the ancient manuscripts of the Gospel of Matthew. Many people believe the Gospel of Matthew was written in Greek. However, an early Christian Father, Papias (AD 60-135), wrote that Matthew "compiled the sayings [of the Lord] in the Aramaic language, and everyone translated them as well as he could."[4] And Eusebius of Caesarea (AD 263-339), known as the "Father of Church History," declared that "Matthew had begun by preaching to the Hebrews, and when he made up his mind to go to others too, he committed

his own Gospel to writing in his native tongue [Aramaic]."[5] Eusebius was a student of another early church leader, Pamphilius of Caesarea (b. unknown d. AD 309). Pamphilius was a dedicated collector of theological writings. His school, library, and scriptorium were considered second only to the ones in Alexandria. At his death, Eusebius inherited Pamphilius's extensive library and scriptorium. (More about this later.)

In addition, a Hebrew Gospel of Matthew, dated in the 14th century, was preserved in a work called Eben Bohan (The Touchstone) by Spanish-Jewish rabbi Shem Tov ben Isacc ben Shaprut. Despite its late date, some, but not all, scholars believe the Jews preserved the Hebrew wording from the first century, as was their meticulous habit regarding Scripture. The Great Commission to the Disciples in Shem Tov's book reads: "Go and teach them to carry out all the things which I have commanded you forever."[6]

It wasn't until the 16th century that the Greek scholar and translator Erasmus argued that Matthew was originally written in Greek, based on the lack of any extant manuscripts in Aramaic or Hebrew.

What Was in the Rare Book Section?

It is estimated there were 30,000 books in the library at Caesarea, curated by Pamphilius and Eusebius. Historians guess the library remained more or less intact until it was destroyed in the 6th century by Muslim warriors. There is no catalog of the actual contents.

However, Jerome (AD 345-420), the translator of the Latin Vulgate, wrote about the original Hebrew copy of the Gospel of Matthew:

> Matthew, also called Levi, apostle and a foretimes publican, composed a gospel of Christ at first published in Judea in Hebrew for the sake of those of the circumcision who believed, but this was afterwards translated into Greek, though by what author is uncertain. The Hebrew itself has been preserved until the present day in have also had the opportunity of having the volume described to me by the Nazarenes of Berœa, a city of Syria, who use it.[7]

So, the question is: Did Eusebius have Matthew's original manuscript at his disposal? He doesn't say so, but he does cite Matthew 28:19 many times using *"in my name"* or something similar. A few examples:

> *Demonstratio Evangelica*, (The Proof of the Gospel) Book 3, 1. 3:6 With one word and voice He said to His disciples: "Go, and make disciples of all the nations in **My Name**, teaching them to observe all things whatsoever I have commanded you." And He joined the effect to His Word;

> *Demonstratio Evangelica*, Book 3, 1. 3:7 Whereas He, who conceived nothing human or mortal, see how truly He speaks with the voice of God, saying in these very words to those disciples of His, the poorest of the poor: "Go forth, and make disciples of all the nations." "But how," the disciples might reasonably have answered the Master, ...But while the disciples of Jesus were most likely either saying thus, or thinking thus, the Master solved their difficulties by the addition of one phrase, saying they should triumph: **"In my name."**

> *Theophania*, Book 4, 24. 4:9 On one occasion indeed, He said that **"in His Name** should be preached repentance to all nations."

Church History, Book 3, 13. 5:2 But the rest of the apostles, who had been incessantly plotted against with a view to their destruction, and had been driven out of the land of Judea, went unto all nations to preach the Gospel, relying upon the power of Christ, who had said to them,— "Go ye and make disciples of all the nations **in My Name.**"

Weak Sauce

Some theologians argue that the Triune language in Matthew 24:19 is the correct wording. They question how a conspiracy to substitute the former language could be pulled off. They also depend on finding the wording in old Matthew manuscripts. However, these are dated only from the fourth century on. While some references in other early church writings mention the Father, Son, and Holy Spirit, these are not Scripture. In addition, the Trinity wording appears in a few copies of Eusebius's writings, but only those dated around his death in 339 and after the Council of Nicea.

This circumstance is not too remarkable, as we know many cultures worshipped a threefold godhead, elaborately detailed in Alexander Hislop's *The Two Babylons*.[8] Threefold washings were a ritual used by these pagan religions long before Christ. This idea may have been introduced into the false church established by the Samaritan, Simon Magus, probably the "Simon" who became the Catholic Church's first Pope, not Simon Peter, as they claim.[9]

Even the Catholic Church, which adopted many pagan Babylonian ideas, admits it changed the wording in Matthew 28:19:

The baptismal formula was changed from the name of Jesus Christ to the words Father, Son, and Holy Spirit by the Catholic Church in the second century... The original formula for baptism was in the Name of Jesus, but the pope changed it.[10]

So, it appears the arguments for baptism in the Father, Son, and Holy Spirit are weak and insubstantial.

The Age of Shadows

The development of the Doctrine of the Trinity evolved over time. It was complex, and there were many players. Jesse Hurlbut, a historian, describes that era:

We name the last generation of the first century, from 68 to AD 100, "The Age of Shadows," partly because the gloom of persecution was over the church, but more especially because of all the periods in the [church's] history, it is the one about which we know the least. We have no longer the clear light of the Book of Acts to guide us; and no author of that age has filled the blank in the history.[11]

Just a few decades after Jesus' resurrection and ascension to heaven, some of the false teachers predicted by the New Testament authors arose.

I know that after my departure savage wolves will come in among you, not sparing the flock; and from among your own selves men will arise, speaking perverse things, to draw away the disciples after them. (Acts 20:29-30).

For the time will come when they will not tolerate sound doctrine; but wanting to have their ears tickled, they will accumulate for themselves teachers in accordance with their own desires, and they will turn their ears away from the truth and will turn aside to myths. (2 Tim 4:3-4).

But false prophets also appeared among the people, just as there will also be false teachers among you, who will secretly introduce destructive heresies, even denying the Master who bought them, bringing swift destruction upon themselves. Many will follow their indecent behavior, and because of them the way of the truth will be maligned. (2 Pet 2:1-2).

During the first years of the Christian age, the true believers were scattered far and wide because of persecution by Roman authorities. The early Christian writings were filled with questions about the nature of Christ. Was he God? Was he a man? Was he a man who changed into a god? Was he a chimera (an illusion)? There were also debates about the Holy Spirit. All this activity occurred in an environment of pagan Babylonian, Greek, and Roman ideas, some of which were attractive to these scholars. Eventually, by the mid-4th century, the disagreement settled down to two main camps, the followers of Arius (non-trinitarian) and those of Athanasius (trinitarian). The debate was fraught with violence. The Trinity dogma required many councils,

threats, deceit, and blood before its consolidation; thousands were put to death during this time. (Many more deaths were to follow during the 1600-year history of Papal reign—millions of Trinity deniers have been found worthy of death.)

An Old Man at the Council of Nicaea
The Roman Emperor, Constantine the Great, was alarmed by the violence of the nature of God debate, a challenge to keeping his empire unified. In AD 325, for political reasons, not religious, he called for all the premier bishops to convene in Nicaea, in modern-day Turkey. Eusebius was one of them. Indeed, he was privileged with a seat on the dais beside Constantine and gave the opening oratory. Even though he leaned toward Arianism, he and the other bishops were cowed by the grandeur of the Emperor into going along with his choice. Constantine did not care what the outcome would be; he just wanted closure and unity. Constantine chose to support the Athanasian position. Eusebius, who, by now, was quite elderly and perhaps not his usual forceful self, reluctantly went along. We know his thoughts because he wrote a letter to his congregation in Caesarea:

This we have been forced to transmit to you, Beloved, as making clear to you the deliberation of our inquiry and assent, and how reasonably we resisted even to the last minute as long as we were offended at statements which differed from our own, but received without contention what no longer pained us, as soon as, on a candid examination of the sense of the words, they appeared to us to coincide with what we ourselves have professed in the faith which we have already published.[12]

The result of the conference was the Nicene Creed, which forms the basis of understanding about God in most of today's Christian religions.[13] Matthew 28:19 is prime proof for believers of the Trinity. What if that language has been changed? How do we rationalize some Bible passages as original and others as not? This question is the elephant in the room, a most difficult question. We encounter it when modern translations use newly discovered and earlier-dated documents. When scholars find wording deviations, both omissions, and additions, they note them in the margins of our Bibles. The length to which we trust in the inclusion of this recently discovered language in modern Bibles is one for further individual study.

So What?

What does it matter that Christadelphians baptize using the Trinity Formula? Does it make the baptism invalid? No. Does it mean we think Jesus is God? Absolutely not. Is God a three-person entity? Again, no! However, some brothers and sisters may be more sensitive to this issue than others and ask why we reference a God we don't believe in. This is a doctrine we take great pains to reject. We make sure our baptism candidates don't espouse the Trinity. It is one of the major differences between our community and other religions. Why would Jesus endorse the Triune God?

If using the Trinitarian Baptism Formula is bothersome, it may be worthwhile to turn to the language used in other baptism scenarios in the New Testament. Why not perform your next baptism with "I baptize you in the **name of Jesus Christ**."

Melinda Flatley,
Pittsburgh Ecclesia, PA

1 Roberts, Robert, The Ecclesial Guide, Birmingham, The Christadelphian, (1989), p. 7.

2 All Scriptural citations are taken from the New American Standard Bible, unless specifically noted.

3 Some scholars believe Mark 16:9-20 might not be in the original. There are pros and cons to this question. See thegospelcoalition.org/article/was-mark-16-9-20-originally-mark-gospel/. In any event, the Triune Formula is not present.

4 Eusebius, History of the Church, Book III, Chap. 39.16.

5 Ibid. Chap. 24.6.

6 Howard, George, The Hebrew Gospel of Matthew, Mercer University Press, 2005.

7 Jerome, De Viris Illustreibus, (On Illustrious Men), #3

8 Hislop, Alexander, The Two Babylons, Partridge, London, 1926.

9 1stcenturychristian.com/SimonMagus.

10 The Catholic Encyclopedia of 1913 (vol. II, pp. 263 and 265).

11 Hurlbut, Jesse, The Story of the Christian Church, 1970. p. 33.

12 Newman, John Henry, Library of the Fathers, vol. 8, pp. 59-72.

13 Wikipedia.org/wiki/Nicene_Creed.

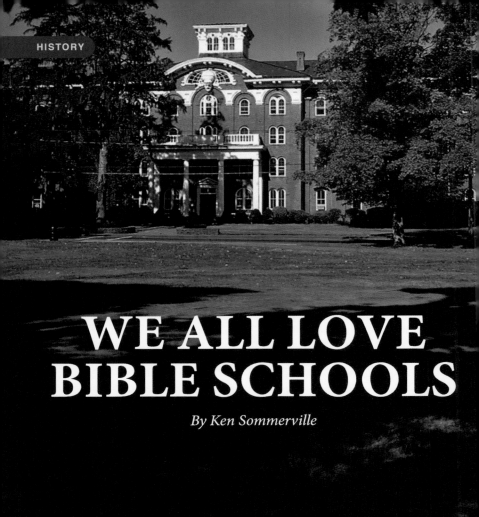

WE ALL LOVE BIBLE SCHOOLS

By Ken Sommerville

THIS year, we've attended three wonderful weeks of Bible School— Palm Springs, Rocky Mountain, and our local Idyllwild Bible School. Bible Schools are an invaluable resource in the Christadelphian community, a blessing to us in so many ways. They affect us deeply, for good and forever.

In 1950, I was about thirteen years old when I attended the Eastern Bible School, my first Bible School. It was located in Wilbraham, Massachusetts. (Wilbraham Academy pictured above.) The school and the friends I made there impacted my life, allowing me to survive my teenage years, and it became a spiritual anchor. Bible Schools have impacted most of our lives spiritually. Some have been baptized at Bible Schools. Some have met their spouse there. We all have benefited from the years of Bible study that our teaching brethren have shared with us in their classes. Brothers and Sisters prepare classes for the children, with crafts and projects that enable our little ones to learn many basic Bible facts and stories. These remain with them for the rest of their lives.

The Idyllwild Pines camp itself was started in 1923, one hundred years ago this year. The facility was created to provide a place for Christian churches to have Bible Schools. Fortunately, it is not owned by one denomination, so we have been allowed to rent it. As some Bible Schools have experienced, many Christian camps dismiss us as a "cult" because we do not believe in the Trinity. The Christadelphians have been meeting there for 68 years, since 1955. My wife, Sis. Bonnie attended the first school and has been going ever since.

The gratitude felt for all the hard work that goes into our Bible Schools caused me to wonder when the first Bible School began and who started this wonderful practice. I had it in the back of my mind that the first Christadelphian Bible School was in Arkansas, sponsored by the Unamended Christadelphians. I discussed this with Bro. Dave Jennings because his mother (now deceased) was originally from that community and learned about the Truth there. It turned out that The Advocate Magazine recently published an article about the school. Dave sent me a copy, and it got things going. The heading for the article is: "One Hundred Years of The Arkansas Bible School." It was the first Bible School in the USA and possibly the first in the world. That Bible School is located in Martinville, Arkansas, which is less than an hour north of Little Rock. The article has many pictures of the camp and some of the participants over the years. Most of the article consists of individual brothers and sisters sharing their personal memories of school.

What follows is not intended to be a definitive history of Christadelphian Bible Schools but rather a sharing of some of the background of a few of the Bible Schools and camps that I, and many of you, have attended over the years.

A Wilbraham/Arkansas Connection

I remembered hearing that Bro. Alvin Brittle (who lived in New Jersey and was very important in my life at some key junctures) had been instrumental in bringing the Arkansas Bible School concept to the Central fellowship, which resulted in the Wilbraham Bible School. Bro. Jim Sullivan in Massachusetts has put together a history of Wilbraham and has given a number of presentations on the subject over the years. He has a copy of "The Origin of the Eastern Christadelphian Bible School" written by Bro. Alvin Brittle. My dim recollection was confirmed. Bro. Alvin was a key factor in getting Wilbraham started. I might also add that he was a factor in the

Group photo of the Eastern Christadephian Bible School at Wilbraham Academy in 1947

Hanover Bible School's beginnings. Alvin leaned into my car as I said goodbye to everyone upon leaving the Orange, New Jersey Ecclesia and moving to the Midwest. He said they really needed a Bible School in the Midwest, and I should start one. The furthest thing from my mind was that I would start a Bible School. I was about twenty-two and only baptized for a year.

Nevertheless, it stuck in my mind, and I shared Alvin's suggestion at a planning meeting after a young people's weekend at the Shakamak State Park in Jasonville, Indiana. The brothers and sisters in Indiana and Illinois took it up and, with God's blessing, got the Hanover Bible School going.

The following is quoted from Bro. Alvin's history of the beginnings of Wilbraham:

> While serving in conscientious objector camps during World War 2, brethren from the Eastern USA learned that years ago there

had been weeklong Bible camps started in Texas by the Berean Fellowship, and in Arkansas by the Advocate fellowship. When they were released from Civilian Public Service in the summer of 1946, Bro. Doug Egles, Bro. Don Lipfert, and Bro. Al Brittle decided to drive out and attend the Arkansas Bible School.

In September 1946, several brothers and sisters got together and decided to start a Bible School in the eastern USA. Sis. Ruth Rankin suggested Wilbraham as a location, as she was working there as an accountant and knew Charles Stevens, the director. A committee was formed, brochures were sent out, and the first Bible School was held the following year. The school ran from August 9 through August 17. There was an advisory group called the "Executive Committee" and a larger group of brethren involved in all the many tasks necessary for a Bible School. One such task was recording the classes, and I remember helping Bro. Howard Wallace by running between classes with the microphones.

Bro. Fred Turner was the first brother to come from England and teach in 1950. Bro. John Carter followed in 1951 and 1952. Those, and some subsequent visits, led to the resolution of the Central and Berean Fellowship division in 1952. The West Coast was almost entirely Berean at that time, and a number of them attended Wilbraham. As a result of the reunion and what they experienced during their visits, these brethren determined to form a Pacific Coast Bible School (Idyllwild).

Emerson Hall at Idyllwild Pines Camp

The Wilbraham Bible School has changed locations since its beginnings. All involved are very thankful God has blessed the school and enabled it to continue.

The Pacific Coast Christadelphian Bible School

Idyllwild began in 1955. Wilbraham influenced its beginnings as the result of some California brothers attending that school. A committee was formed, including Bro. Bob Lloyd, who, at that time, was the youngest brother on the committee. Sis. Peggy Lloyd, who attended that first Bible School, assisted me with some of the early recollections.

As we mentioned at the outset, this year, 2023, is the 100th

anniversary of the camp and the 68th. anniversary of our Bible School being held at the camp. It is located about a three-hour drive southeast of Los Angeles, in the San Jacinto Mountains, at 5,000 ft. elevation. It is a very beautiful location. The San Jacinto Mountain range is the second highest in California, reaching 10,804 feet at its peak.

The campgrounds and facilities have been expanded and improved in many ways over the years to the benefit of us all. The original camp had no cabins

Brethren Mansfield, Whittaker and Wubbels at Idyllwild Bible School in 1960

in the meadow and did not include the 40 acres of a neighboring Jewish Camp called "Gilboa." The addition of Gilboa added classrooms and cabins. The camp initially consisted of what we now refer to as "the upper camp," and the sleeping facilities were called "the chicken coops." Two families would be in one chicken coop, separated by a hanging curtain. I remember when a family sharing our cabin had one of their children get sick in the middle of the night. The following day, on the way to breakfast, the father apologized for all the noise. I told him not to worry. I was so thankful that it wasn't one of ours and that the noise didn't bother me a bit.

The format of the school week is typical of most Bible Schools. Three classes in the morning for the adults, three for the teens, and classes for the children, along with a nursery group. There were about 350 adults and children in attendance this year. Recruiting all the teachers kept Sis. Jennifer Russell extremely busy. The teachers prepared their lessons and crafts, and Sis. Kristin Atwood and others helped the children prepare for their musical presentations at the end of the week.

Sis. Kristin also led the choral practice every afternoon, and the choral presentation was one of the high points at the end of the week. There are many other activities for all the different age groups, all of which take planning and guidance. It is a lot of work, for which we are all very thankful.

Sadly, there is a downside to the Idyllwild location, which is the danger of wildfires. One year, we couldn't go up the hill at all because of fires. Another year, we had to come home because of fires that endangered the camp. Fortunately, the camp and the town of Idyllwild have been spared. In both years, there were fires. The Bible School Committee pivoted and held the classes at the Simi Hills Ecclesial Hall. Brothers and sisters from other areas stayed at the homes of local brothers and sisters for the rest of the week.

Western Bible School

The first Bible School in the West was the Western Bible School, started in 1951 by the Unamended Christadelphians. The first location was in the Lake Tahoe area, later moving to Boulder Creek, near Santa Cruz, about thirty miles southwest of San Jose, CA. The brethren had to change locations several times, as the camps would determine that our beliefs were incompatible with theirs. In 1969, they moved to the Menucha Retreat and Conference Center in Corbett, Oregon, about thirty miles east of Portland. The Bible School continues to meet at the same location.

The Hawksworths and the Gravelees at the Western Bible School in 1959

Calaveras

During the early 1960s, some Unamended families living in the Modesto and Merced areas in California began gathering at the Calaveras Big Trees State Park (east of Sacramento) for a week. It was an affordable location. It did not start out as a Bible School, per se, but eventually it became one. I recall when Bro. Harry Whitaker taught at the camp for one year. Mark Twain's short story about the frog-jumping contest made the Calaveras area famous, which I believe is still re-enacted each year. It is a beautiful location with ideal weather for camping. We all had tents in those days. I remember one family's campsite consisted of a clothesline strung around four trees, with blankets hanging over them. Cooking was in the firepit and on camp stoves. There were three classes in the morning and afternoon, after which we drove down to the beautiful and refreshing Stanislaus River.

Sharin' Woods

After some years at Calaveras, the camp moved to Sharin' Woods. Bro. Ron and Sis. Dee Magness bought forty acres in the mountains near Shaver Lake, where they and their son and daughter-in-law, Bro. Leonard and Sis. Beth Magness could also have a home. The idea was that there would be plenty of room for the Bible Camp, and it really served us well. We would continue our classes in the morning, and in the afternoon, many would go to nearby Shaver Lake. We would also have gatherings there over the Memorial Day and Labor Day weekends.

The fact that we were there representing two different fellowships brought home to all of us on Sundays when we would have two different Breaking of Bread services going on in two distinct parts of the camp. We were far apart enough that we could not see each other but could hear each other singing the hymns. The plus side to all this experience was that we got to know, love, respect each other, and share our love and knowledge of the Scriptures. With God's blessing, that was no small factor in enabling our doctrinal differences to be reasoned out and for us to come to a oneness of mind when the reunion efforts began.

Sadly, Sharin' Woods ended after thirteen years, but the contributions it made to us spiritually lives on. Interestingly, in different ways, both Wilbraham and the California Bible camps were important components in unifying much of the community.

The Feast of Booths

Bonnie and I have been to nearly ten different Bible Schools over the years. There are many more in North America and in other countries. We have just touched on a bit of the history and the many features we appreciate in our Bible Schools and how distinctive features have affected us at various stages in our lives.

Bible School week is a holy week. While we are there, we are completely separated from the World. It makes one think of the Feast of Booths under the Law. The Feast of Booths was the most joyful of Israel's feasts. While we usually think of Israel's feasts as solemn occasions, this was much more like a campout with your family and all the other families nearby. The purpose was to cause them to remember that for forty years, God sustained them as they lived in "booths" while they wandered in the wilderness. Each succeeding generation was taught in this powerful, week-long experience.

Also in the fifteenth day of the seventh month, when ye have gathered in the fruit of the land, ye shall keep a feast unto the LORD seven days: on the first day shall be a sabbath, and on the eighth day shall be a sabbath. And ye shall take you on the first day the boughs of goodly trees, branches of palm trees, and the boughs of thick trees, and willows of the brook; and ye shall rejoice before the LORD your God seven days. And ye shall keep it a feast unto the LORD seven days in the year. It shall be a statute for ever in your generations: ye shall celebrate it in the seventh month Ye shall dwell in booths seven days; all that are Israelites born shall dwell in booths: That your generations may know that I made the children of Israel to dwell in booths, when I brought them out of the land of Egypt: I am the LORD your God. And Moses declared unto the children of Israel the feasts of the LORD." (Lev. 23:39-44).

Conclusion

Attending a Bible School is the ideal family vacation. There are activities planned for all ages. I can't think of any place where you can take your young family and have something that appeals to each of them at their stage of development. As you pull up to the camp and open the car doors, the kids are gone in a flash, looking for their friends. It is so much more than just one week.

We look forward to Bible School all year and remember it all our lives. We pray God will continue to bless us with our Bible Schools as we prepare ourselves and our blessed children for His Son's return. May it be soon.

Ken Sommerville,
Simi Hills Ecclesia, CA

A long tradition of Bible Schools has blessed the Christadelphian community

BOOK REVIEW

CHRIST BEFORE CREEDS
REDISCOVERING THE JESUS OF HISTORY
Written by Jeff Deuble

Reviewed by Chris Sales

I N *"Christ before Creeds,"* Jeff Deuble recounts his own personal journey of discovery from Trinitarian Pastor to Unitarian Bible student. That journey involved intense Bible study, much soul searching, and a willingness to look again at many of his own long-standing beliefs. It was indeed a matter of "rediscovering" a man the author thought he already knew. Perhaps another way to phrase the subtitle would have been "Rediscovering the Jesus of the Bible!"

This well-written, easy-to-read, and relatively short (less than 200 pages) book gives a concise yet thorough look at the key principles involved in this topic. Deuble powerfully outlines the development of the doctrine of the Trinity, showing that the Jewish Old Testament and the Christian New Testament speak nothing of this doctrine. His research is sound, and he gives lots of footnotes to allow the reader to check it out for themselves if desired. Appendix B also lists many of the resources he used.

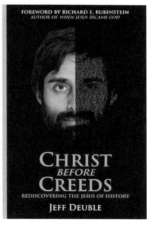

His reasoning from Scripture is also sound, and much of what he says would be welcomed from any Christadelphian platform on the topic of the nature of God and Jesus. In fact, he offers some ideas that I will have to add to my notes on the topic! That is because this account is from the perspective of someone who believed and preached the Trinity and gives insights that many Christadelphians (including myself) could never have seen for themselves.

The first six chapters comprise the bulk of the book, covering the main teaching component, and are all framed as questions: "Why This Book?" "Why Bother?" Why Question?" "What Went Wrong?" "What Does The Bible Teach?" and "Who Is Jesus?" Deuble answers each of these questions in a compelling way and manages to do it without rhetoric or condescension. And he does so in a very succinct manner, without getting bogged down in the usual "rabbit-holes" that arise in such discussions. He is also not overly technical but allows the Scriptures to speak for themselves, showing how a non-Trinitarian view is much more consistent with the overall teaching about God the Father and the agency of His Son, the Lord Jesus Christ.

Each chapter ends with a nice summary of the key points, making the book even better as a teaching tool. Here are some snippets from the "Who Is Jesus?" chapter summary.

> The Bible declares why Jesus is unique in so many ways–the perfect reflection he is of God, the special place he holds in God's heart and purposes for the world, the ideal example he is of how we are meant to live and what we are destined to be.

> The Bible teaches that this Jesus came as a human being in the flesh. He was born and lived as a man: completely human.

> A [Trinitarian] Jesus would not be genuinely and authentically human. Hence, he could not be truly mortal, tempted and tested, perfected, capable of completely identifying and sympathizing with us. He would be less fully the model, mediator, pioneer, perfecter, brother, and High Priest that the Bible declares him to be.

A brief comment about the "What's Essential?" chapter, where the author basically asks, "Does it matter if we believe differently on this topic?" As Christadelphians, we would say that it certainly does. However, this chapter is still worth reading even though Deuble argues for a closer association and fellowship between those that believe in the Trinity and those that don't. Having been ostracized and kicked out of his own church, he makes a strong case for finding a kinder way to handle disputes in the church.

Appendix A is like a "wrested scriptures" on the topic and gives insights and arguments I have not read or thought of before—a great addition to any Christadelphian lecture or Bible Class.

Summary

Even as non-Trinitarians, this book is well worth reading by Christadelphians. It is also a book I plan to give to my Trinitarian friends that could be much more powerful for them, coming from "one of their own." Jeff Deuble gives a powerful testimony in defense of a non-Trinitarian model of the relationship between God and Jesus and what that means for us as believers. This is perhaps the best account that I have ever read of why the Trinity is not Biblical and why Jesus is the "Son of God," not "God the Son."

I will leave you with Deuble's own final plea on the subject.

Rediscover the Jesus of the Bible–to remove the overlays of subsequent Greek philosophical thinking… to return to a more genuine and Jewish Jesus, a more historic, holistic, and human Jesus, a less creedal and a more credible Jesus, as truly portrayed in the Scriptures.

Chris Sales,
Collingwood Ecclesia, ON

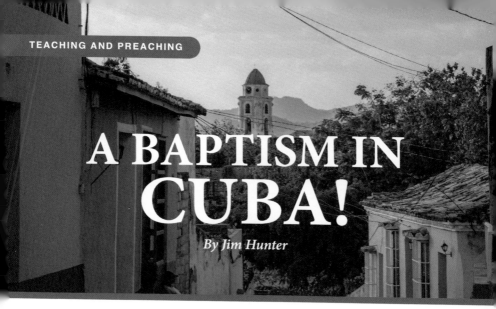

A BAPTISM IN CUBA!

By Jim Hunter

WE are happy to announce that on September 17, 2023, in Bayamo, Cuba, Yoandris Pompa Valdespino was baptized into the Hope of Israel. Five and a half years ago, he began searching the web for a community that studied the Bible. Yoandris came across labiblia.com and requested the postal course. He has been studying with us since, first by mail until the service was interrupted, and afterward, mainly by Skype and WhatsApp. He is a delightful young man with a lovely wife, Lisnet, a neonatal nurse. They have three sons aged ten, eight, and four. We believe this to be the first baptism in the Truth in Cuba.

It took some time to navigate the problem of a US resident trying to travel to Cuba. On the day of the baptism, Yoandris and I had to travel up and down the river, which flows through the city, to find a stretch deep enough for him to be immersed in. Afterward, Lisnet provided lunch at the house and Bro. Yoandris and I celebrated a memorial service, where I received him into fellowship, and we broke bread together. May our Heavenly Father bless and guide our new brother in his walk to the Kingdom

Jim Hunter,
CBMA Link for Cuba

TRUTH CORPS 2023

by Cassie Giordano

We've got good news of the Kingdom of God.
We've got good news of the Kingdom of God.
We will reign with Jesus
as a kingdom of priests!
We will teach the nations!
Hallelujah!
Serving! Serving!
We will all be serving in the Kingdom of God.

It's the last day as Truth Corps team leaders this summer, and the walls of the little May Pen Ecclesial meeting room reverberate with exuberant voices singing Bre. James DiLiberto and Phil Rosser's upbeat song. The lyrics express vivid descriptions from the Scriptures about what life will be like for us when Christ returns. Lines about the desert blooming like the rose and the lame leaping like a deer never fail to move me, and overall, the lyrics seem a perfect fit for our efforts over the previous weeks. Truth Corps is all about preparing young brothers and sisters to spread the Gospel, the Good News of the Kingdom, and putting it into practice. It's also about being servants to ecclesias who want help with efforts they hope will fuel growth in their membership.

On this day, our small group is just nine or ten Jamaicans, six team members, and three leaders. It could easily have been a discouraging start to the little vacation Bible school that was beginning that day. Still, it's impossible not to find a bit of optimism after feeling the energy our closing singing round brought. With only three students on the first day, our expectations were low, but on Tuesday, participation had quadrupled and stayed steady to the end of the week. On Friday, even a few community members showed up for a public lecture! We were glad some results came from our canvassing around the neighborhood the previous week.

Due to some snags getting Truth Corps up and running after our long COVID hiatus, a promising contingent of volunteers dwindled away while plans were in limbo. In the end, we only had two team members available to travel to Jamaica for two weeks and another two joining us during the second week, so spreading the word about upcoming events was left in the hands of just a few of us, with the help of ecclesial members.

Thankfully, we had time to do some preparation for canvassing before we left the US. Sis. Sydney Pittman and Bro. Judah Lange are members of Norfolk, our home ecclesia, and we were blessed to have the opportunity to spend time with them the week before we traveled, practicing how to approach strangers and try to engage them in conversation about our upcoming Learn to Read the Bible Effectively Seminar. With the help of two other CYC members, we visited a few parks in the area and were pleasantly surprised with how many people responded positively to being approached. At least as many people accepted a flyer as rejected it, and it left us feeling inspired to carry on with canvassing activities as an ecclesia in the future. Hanging around outdoors in Virginia's summer humidity also felt like good preparation for the climate in Jamaica!

Then, it was time to apply what we'd practiced far from home. Once we'd picked up our rental car, we drove the long boulder-lined causeway that links the airport to Kingston proper, skirted Kingston and went to Free Town, where Bro. Leroy and Sis. Loraine Johnson live. We were exhausted but thrilled to see how comfortably things were arranged for us. Between sleep deprivation and the heat, most of us headed right to bed for a nap before supper so that we'd be reasonably recovered by the Memorial Service the next day. Being tired and overheated was something of a theme for our first week, as even by the standards of our local brethren, the weather was hot. Thankfully, we were only scheduled to canvas in the morning heat one day, and everything else was done in the late afternoon when the sun was a bit less fierce. With ecclesial assistance, we distributed all the fliers we brought with us by Wednesday and filled the rest of our time enjoying Bible readings, devotions, and first principles workshops with the Johnson family. Bro. Lorenzo and Bro. Okeimo Johnson were able to participate as full team members with us during these activities and presented workshops and devotions for us as well, providing mutual benefit for all involved.

Our remaining team members began arriving that Saturday, and by Sunday night, we had a team of four, plus three team leaders. What a difference in energy that made! Sis. Loraine made us a phenomenal supper that evening, and we had eleven people sitting around a table feasting on chicken, rice and peas, potato salad, pasta salad, pear (avocado to us), and more. The conversation barely let up through cleanup and carried right on into the Bible readings, and we finished the evening with my favorite activity once again: singing together. The extra voices made such a difference, and I couldn't help but reflect on the integral part that singing played in the three other Truth Corps teams we've worked with as leaders and my own two trips as a team member many years ago. The years may pass, but the joy of singing and speaking about God's word never fades for me. It felt like the right way to end our time in May Pen. In the morning, we had one more chance to raise our voices together at the VBS, and then it was time to say goodbye, with the words "We've got good news" still ringing in my head. After all, bringing that good news is what it's all about, on Truth Corps and every day in our lives.

Cassie Giordano,
Norfolk Ecclesia, VA,
Truth Corps Leader Team

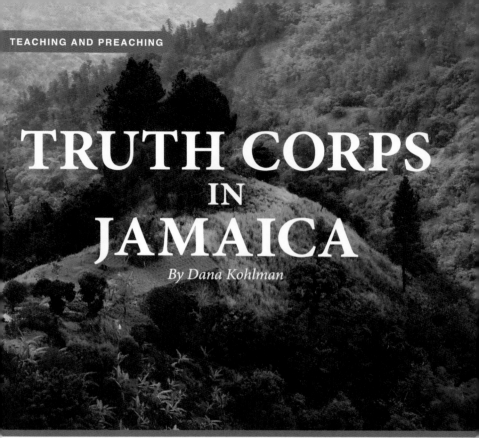

TRUTH CORPS
IN
JAMAICA
By Dana Kohlman

TRUTH Corps 2023 was deeply positive for the May Pen ecclesia, the Truth Corps team, and the young Sunday School attendees who participated in the Vacation Bible School (VBS). More than anything, I suspect the success could be attributed to a combination of some very solid team members and a very strong host family.

The team stayed at the home of the Johnson family. The Johnsons are remarkable. They provided excellent accommodations, relentless hospitality, catering, and great fellowship. I suspect, for the young people, the Johnsons were the strongest support as they provided the most learning (both Sis. Lorraine and Bro. Leroy are staunch Bible students) and Scriptural engagement. We had lively discussions around the readings with them, and many follow-up engaging conversations followed.

The team itself, while small, was deeply rich. Having the two Johnson boys with us, Okeimo and Lorenzo, may have contributed most substantially to this. Both boys participated in the VBS classes. All of the team activities were game for any extracurricular activities and often led the way.

I was thrilled to see the heavy lifting of the North American young people. It would take a lot of work to find a way to infuse more learning into the VBS. Sis. Sydney Pitman, Sis. Jane Kohlman and Bro. Judah Lange were all in during their lessons with the students. Bro. Erick Cervantes and I covered the teen classes, and the folks who were in the room supported us with some lively commentary. Every time I looked into the younger class, it was a "hive" of learning.

The team benefited from the presence and leadership of Bro. Erick Cervantes. It is hard to replace young, enthusiastic brothers willing to do this sort of work. Bro. Erick is such a great example to young people.

Overall, the experience, while blisteringly hot, benefited everyone. Work in developing countries is exhausting work. It's an emotional labor as well. We live in distorted circumstances in the West. Most of us take the opportunities surrounding us for granted: safe neighborhoods, access to a robust economy, a moderate climate, and legal accountability. Getting up close to the poverty surrounding most of the world is grounding.

The greatest strength of Truth Corps is that it allows young people to have these experiences and support our community. Hopefully, we all recognize the ties that bind us. God's call to righteousness transcends the wickedness, inequity, and disorder that make so much of the rest of the world.

Meeting with brothers and sisters who love and understand the calling of Scripture, despite difficult circumstances, encourages those of us in the West, surrounded by perennial indulgence, to stay grounded and appreciate the abundance we've been blessed with. Hopefully, we can leverage our privilege into greater service. It's hard to ignore Paul's directive in Romans 14:17 that the Kingdom is *"about righteousness, peace and joy."*

Please consider contacting Truth Corps contacts in your area to get information and encourage young people to volunteer some of their summer to support this worthy work. As part of your CYC or Bible class, I strongly recommend you have a "Zoom" session with Truth Corps alumni to get some insights and encouragement to join or support in other ways.

Dana Kohlman,
Calgary Ecclesia, AB
Truth Corps Leader

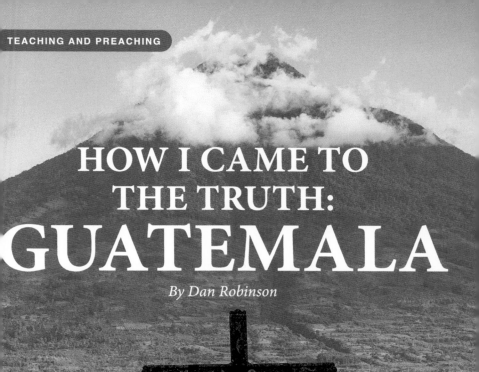

HOW I CAME TO THE TRUTH: GUATEMALA

By Dan Robinson

Sis. Ruth Noemí Trinidad Guzmán

I was baptized in 2019 at the Bible School that is held in El Salvador. My father is Bro. Jorge Trinidad. I am 24 years old, and very grateful that God has chosen me to be part of His family. I am happy to be part of the Christadelphian community since I have found people who really live according to what God has revealed in the Bible. My biggest goal is to live a life in line with God's purpose for me, and by my example, to encourage some of those close to me to find the truth as I have.

Bro. Jorge Trinidad

When I found the Christadelphians, I thought they would be the same as the Evangelical churches I had been a part of, expecting they would teach me the same things. However, I was incredibly surprised to learn that I needed a correct understanding of the Scriptures. It is for this reason that I have remained with my Christadelphian family since the year 2000.

Bro. Victor Leonel Garcia

While looking for employment, I found an advertisement in the newspaper placed by the Christadelphian Bible Mission announcing free Bible correspondence courses. I sent in my name and address and began to receive the Bible studies. This was how I came to know the Christadelphian Bible Mission and learned the truth through the Bible. I have now been baptized for eight years.

Bro. Juan Palacios

I came to know the Christadelphian ecclesia by means of an advertisement in the newspaper.

Bro. Victor Leonel Garcia, and Sis. Marina Velasquez de Garcia

As a couple, we arrived at the Christadelphian Bible Mission with an understanding of the Bible but not with a knowledge of the Truth. By means of the Bible studies we received, we learned the Truth. As we do everything as a couple, we were baptized on the same day and have persevered. We have helped our children and grandchildren learn the Truth of the Bible. During our time on this earth, our mission is to take the message of salvation to a world in need. Our desire is to fulfill the words of our Lord Jesus in Mark 16:15, "And he said unto them, Go ye into all the world, and preach the gospel to every creature."

Sis. Zully Salazar

I was baptized on August 5, 2001, in Guatemala City. Bro. Douglas Vanegas gave me baptismal classes and baptized me. Bro. Ed Binch arrived, along with other brethren from El Salvador, and gave the exhortation. I was gifted a Bible that I still have.

Dan Robinson,
Brampton Ecclesia, ON
CBMA Link for Guatemala

Sis. Victoria Garcia

I learned from my parents, Victor and Marina! I attended a lecture, and it was interesting to me. Thus, I began a journey towards the Truth. From the first day I arrived at the ecclesia, I felt part of the family of Christ! It is never too late to start again and continue advancing step by step!

Acatenango, Dipartimento di
Chimaltenango, Guatemala

THE CHRISTADELPHIAN
TIDINGS
OF THE KINGDOM OF GOD

is published monthly, except bimonthly in July-August, by The **Christadelphian Tidings**, 567 Astorian Drive, Simi Valley, CA 93065-5941. **FIRST CLASS POSTAGE PAID** at Simi Valley, CA and at additional mailing offices. POSTMASTER: Send address changes to The Christadelphian Tidings, 567 Astorian Dr., Simi Valley, CA 93065.

Christadelphian Tidings Publishing Committee: Alan Markwith (Chairman), Joe Hill, John Bilello, Peter Bilello, Linda Beckerson, Nancy Brinkerhoff, Shawn Moynihan, Kevin Flatley, Jeff Gelineau, William Link, and Ken Sommerville.

Christadelphian Tidings Editorial Committee: Dave Jennings (Editor), Section Editors: Nathan Badger (Life Application), TBA (Exhortation and Consolation), Jessica Gelineau (Music and Praise), Steve Cheetham (Exposition), Richard Morgan (First Principles), Dave Jennings (Teaching and Preaching), Jan Berneau (CBMA/C), George Booker, (Thoughts on the Way, Q&A), John Bilello (Letters to the Editor), Jeff Gelineau (News and Notices, Subscriptions), Melinda Flatley (Writer Recruitment and Final Copy), and Shawn Moynihan (Books).

Subscriptions: The Tidings Magazine is provided **FREE** for any who would like to read it. The Magazine is available in PDF Format online at **tidings.org**. If you would like to order a printed subscription to **The Tidings** you may do so simply by making a donation to cover the printing costs. The Suggested Donation for printing and shipping is **USD $70.00;** (we ask for a Minimum Donation of USD $35.00 for a printed subscription.)

All subscription information is available online at **www.tidings.org**. You may subscribe online and make donations online or by mail to the above address. Information on how to subscribe in other countires is also available online at **www.tidings.org/subscribe**.

The Christadelphian Tidings is published on the 15th of the month for the month following. Items for publication must be received by the 1st of the month. Correspondence to the editor, Dave Jennings at **editor@tidings.org**. Publication of articles does not presume editorial endorsement except on matters of fundamental doctrine as set forth in the BASF. Letters should be sent via email to **letters@tidings.org**. Please include your name, address and phone number. The magazine reserves the right to edit all submissions for length and clarity.

Printed in Great Britain
by Amazon

29811423R00043